Modern Language Association of America

Approaches to Teaching
World Literature

Joseph Gibaldi, Series Editor

1. Joseph Gibaldi, ed. *Approaches to Teaching Chaucer's* Canterbury Tales. 1980.
2. Carole Slade, ed. *Approaches to Teaching Dante's* Divine Comedy. 1982.
3. Richard Bjornson, ed. *Approaches to Teaching Cervantes'* Don Quixote. 1984.
4. Jess B. Bessinger, Jr., and Robert F. Yeager, eds. *Approaches to Teaching* Beowulf. 1984.
5. Richard J. Dunn, ed. *Approaches to Teaching Dickens'* David Copperfield. 1984.
6. Steven G. Kellman, ed. *Approaches to Teaching Camus's* The Plague. 1985.
7. Yvonne Shafer, ed. *Approaches to Teaching Ibsen's* A Doll House. 1985.
8. Martin Bickman, ed. *Approaches to Teaching Melville's* Moby-Dick. 1985.
9. Miriam Youngerman Miller and Jane Chance, eds. *Approaches to Teaching* Sir Gawain and the Green Knight. 1986.
10. Galbraith M. Crump, ed. *Approaches to Teaching Milton's* Paradise Lost. 1986.
11. Spencer Hall, with Jonathan Ramsey, eds. *Approaches to Teaching Wordsworth's* Poetry. 1986.
12. Robert H. Ray, ed. *Approaches to Teaching Shakespeare's* King Lear. 1986.
13. Kostas Myrsiades, ed. *Approaches to Teaching Homer's* Iliad *and* Odyssey. 1987.
14. Douglas J. McMillan, ed. *Approaches to Teaching Goethe's* Faust. 1987.
15. Renée Waldinger, ed. *Approaches to Teaching Voltaire's* Candide. 1987.
16. Bernard Koloski, ed. *Approaches to Teaching Chopin's* The Awakening. 1988.
17. Kenneth M. Roemer, ed. *Approaches to Teaching Momaday's* The Way to Rainy Mountain. 1988.
18. Edward J. Rielly, ed. *Approaches to Teaching Swift's* Gulliver's Travels. 1988.
19. Jewel Spears Brooker, ed. *Approaches to Teaching Eliot's Poetry and Plays.* 1988.
20. Melvyn New, ed. *Approaches to Teaching Sterne's* Tristram Shandy. 1989.
21. Robert F. Gleckner and Mark L. Greenberg, eds. *Approaches to Teaching Blake's* Songs of Innocence and of Experience. 1989.
22. Susan J. Rosowski, ed. *Approaches to Teaching Cather's* My Ántonia. 1989.
23. Carey Kaplan and Ellen Cronan Rose, eds. *Approaches to Teaching Lessing's* The Golden Notebook. 1989.
24. Susan Resneck Parr and Pancho Savery, eds. *Approaches to Teaching Ellison's* Invisible Man. 1989.
25. Barry N. Olshen and Yael S. Feldman, eds. *Approaches to Teaching the Hebrew Bible as Literature in Translation.* 1989.
26. Robin Riley Fast and Christine Mack Gordon, eds. *Approaches to Teaching Dickinson's Poetry.* 1989.
27. Spencer Hall, ed. *Approaches to Teaching Shelley's Poetry.* 1990.

28. Sidney Gottlieb, ed. *Approaches to Teaching the Metaphysical Poets.* 1990.

29. Richard K. Emmerson, ed. *Approaches to Teaching Medieval English Drama.* 1990.

30. Kathleen Blake, ed. *Approaches to Teaching Eliot's* Middlemarch. 1990.

31. María Elena de Valdés and Mario J. Valdés, eds. *Approaches to Teaching García Márquez's* One Hundred Years of Solitude. 1990.

32. Donald D. Kummings, ed. *Approaches to Teaching Whitman's* Leaves of Grass. 1990.

33. Stephen C. Behrendt, ed. *Approaches to Teaching Shelley's* Frankenstein. 1990.

34. June Schlueter and Enoch Brater, eds. *Approaches to Teaching Beckett's* Waiting for Godot. 1991.

35. Walter H. Evert and Jack W. Rhodes, eds. *Approaches to Teaching Keats's Poetry.* 1991.

36. Frederick W. Shilstone, ed. *Approaches to Teaching Byron's Poetry.* 1991.

37. Bernth Lindfors, ed. *Approaches to Teaching Achebe's* Things Fall Apart. 1991.

38. Richard E. Matlak, ed. *Approaches to Teaching Coleridge's Poetry and Prose.* 1991.

39. Shirley Geok-lin Lim, ed. *Approaches to Teaching Kingston's* The Woman Warrior. 1991.

40. Maureen Fries and Jeanie Watson, eds. *Approaches to Teaching the Arthurian Tradition.* 1992.

41. Maurice Hunt, ed. *Approaches to Teaching Shakespeare's* The Tempest *and Other Late Romances.* 1992.

42. Diane Long Hoeveler and Beth Lau, eds. *Approaches to Teaching Brontë's* Jane Eyre. 1993.

43. Jeffrey B. Berlin, ed. *Approaches to Teaching Mann's* Death in Venice *and Other Short Fiction.* 1992.

44. Kathleen McCormick and Erwin R. Steinberg, eds. *Approaches to Teaching Joyce's* Ulysses. 1993.

45. Marcia McClintock Folsom, ed. *Approaches to Teaching Austen's* Pride and Prejudice. 1993.

46. Wallace Jackson and R. Paul Yoder, eds. *Approaches to Teaching Pope's Poetry.* 1993.

47. Edward Kamens, ed. *Approaches to Teaching Murasaki Shikibu's* The Tale of Genji. 1993.

48. Patrick Henry, ed. *Approaches to Teaching Montaigne's* Essays. 1994.

49. David R. Anderson and Gwin J. Kolb, eds. *Approaches to Teaching the Works of Samuel Johnson.* 1993.

50. David Lee Miller and Alexander Dunlop, eds. *Approaches to Teaching Spenser's* Faerie Queene. 1994.

Approaches to Teaching Ellison's
Invisible Man

Edited by

Susan Resneck Parr
and
Pancho Savery

The Modern Language Association of America
New York   1989

Library of Congress Cataloging-in-Publication Data

Approaches to teaching Ellison's Invisible man / edited by Susan
    Resneck Parr and Pancho Savery.
        p.   cm. — (Approaches to teaching world literature ; 21)
    Bibliography: p.
    Includes index.
    ISBN 0-87352-505-1   ISBN 0-87352-506-X (pbk.)
    1. Ellison, Ralph. Invisible man.   2. Ellison, Ralph—Study and
teaching.   I. Parr, Susan Resneck.   II. Pancho, Savery, 1950–   .
III. Series.
PS3555.L625I5326   1989
813'.54—dc19   88-13786

A version of David L. Vanderwerken's essay "Focusing on the Prologue and the
Epilogue" appeared in *CCTE Proceedings* 49 (1984): 19–23. Used with
permission.
Susan Resneck Parr's study guide appeared in her book *The Moral of the Story:
Literature, Values, and American Education.* Copyright © 1982 by Teachers
College, Columbia University. Used by permission of Teachers College Press,
Columbia University.

Cover illustration of the paperback edition: detail of Romare Bearden, *The Street,*
collage, 1964. Used with the kind permission of Mrs. Robert M. Benjamin.
Geoffrey Clements, photographer.

Third printing 1994

Published by The Modern Language Association of America
10 Astor Place, New York, New York, 10003-6981

CONTENTS

PREFACE TO THE SERIES

In *The Art of Teaching* Gilbert Highet wrote, "Bad teaching wastes a great deal of effort, and spoils many lives which might have been full of energy and happiness." All too many teachers have failed in their work, Highet argued, simply "because they have not thought about it." We hope that the Approaches to Teaching World Literature series, sponsored by the Modern Language Association's Committee on Teaching and Related Professional Activities, will not only improve the craft—as well as the art—of teaching but also encourage serious and continuing discussion of the aims and methods of teaching literature.

The principal objective of the series is to collect within each volume different points of view on teaching a specific literary work, a literary tradition, or a writer widely taught at the undergraduate level. The preparation of each volume begins with a wide-ranging survey of instructors, thus enabling us to include in the volume the philosophies and approaches, thoughts and methods of scores of experienced teachers. The result is a sourcebook of material, information, and ideas on teaching the subject of the volume to undergraduates.

The series is intended to serve nonspecialists as well as specialists, inexperienced as well as experienced teachers, graduate students who wish to learn effective ways of teaching as well as senior professors who wish to compare their own approaches with the approaches of colleagues in other schools. Of course, no volume in the series can ever substitute for erudition, intelligence, creativity, and sensitivity in teaching. We hope merely that each book will point readers in useful directions; at most each will offer only a first step in the long journey to successful teaching.

Joseph Gibaldi
Series Editor

PREFACE TO THE VOLUME

The process of designating certain texts as worthy of study—as the Modern Language Association has done with its development of the Approaches to Teaching World Literature series—inevitably raises questions about the values that reside in and perhaps even determine our view of literature. These questions are of special interest to those who reject the notion of a canon and who are seeking criteria by which to include in—or exclude from—the courses they teach certain texts, ideas, and methodologies. Indeed, a growing number of teachers and students alike have come to reject the notion that some texts are so inherently valuable and universally significant that they transcend time, place, and individual (or even cultural) preferences. Rather, the argument goes, the assigning of value and significance to particular texts is merely the product of social, political, and cultural biases. The claim that only texts which have endured through time are appropriate subjects for serious study has become equally suspect.

As coeditors of *Approaches to Teaching Ellison's* Invisible Man, Pancho Savery and I faced these questions and several others. For instance, as we considered the best way to shape this volume, we repeatedly asked ourselves whether *Invisible Man* should be valued primarily as a work with universal implications, as an example of the best that the American literary tradition offers, or as a representative of black American fiction. Such questions of course gave birth to others. Has the novel fulfilled the narrator's reach for universality —"Who knows but that, on the lower frequencies, I speak for you?" (*Invisible Man*, 568)? Does the narrator's existential posture—the basis for his belief in his own universality—in some way diminish the social and political problems that the novel also dramatizes? Or, given that these social and political problems are neither fictive nor distant in time, to what extent are they at the heart of the novel's power? Moreover, should the novel be judged in aesthetic terms or in sociopolitical ones? And in the light of these questions, what approach should teachers of the novel take?

Such questions clearly informed the responses of those teachers who contributed to this volume, both in their answers to the survey questions that in great part dictated the content of this book and in the essays themselves. But even more significant to us is that in actual classrooms, these questions seem to be overshadowed by the engagement of both teachers and students in the extraordinary richness of the novel. Thus, teacher after teacher reported that they approach the novel eclectically, dealing with it thematically, structurally, symbolically, historically, politically. They teach the novel in courses on American literature, Afro-American literature, literary "master-pieces," and ethnic literature, as well as in interdisciplinary, sociology, political science, and history courses. They teach it at introductory, advanced, and graduate levels. Although each contributor to the volume has focused on a particular way to enter the novel, in their actual classrooms their approaches are more comprehensive. It is, in fact, difficult to imagine any teacher of *Invisible Man* who does not take into account the topics of most of the essays. In general, the contributors present the substance of what is taught rather than a particular pedagogy, probably because *Invisible Man* is typically located in survey courses where the pedagogy is determined not by the novel itself but rather by the instructor's more general pedagogical preferences.

The history of this volume itself illustrates some of the more difficult and important questions about how the novel should be approached. In the early stages of the project's evolution, the MLA staff made its own (perhaps unconscious) statement about how *Invisible Man* should be taught by sending out questionnaires to the relatively small number of MLA members who listed themselves as teaching ethnic literature rather than to the larger number who identified their field as American literature. Since the mailing yielded only a few responses, Pancho Savery and I sent additional copies of the questionnaire to, and solicited essays from, a wider array of faculty members, including both those who worked primarily within the field of black literature and those who would define themselves more broadly as Americanists. We also sought contributions from teachers at a variety of institutions, and indeed the book represents the work of teachers from small private colleges and from larger comprehensive universities (both public and private) located throughout the country. After we submitted the manuscript for review, its external readers differed about the appropriate emphasis of the essays. Thus, one reader asked for more essays by black contributors, a second hoped for more essays that reflected current theoretical trends, and a third desired more study guides and more attention to innovative teaching. Such a variety of responses in itself speaks to the novel's complexities and richness.

In the light of these considerations, we decided to try to put together a volume of essays that would give the diverse group of teachers who find *Invisible Man* worthy of study the insights that other, equally diverse teachers have gained as they have taught it. In short, we tried to represent as many approaches to the novel as we could. We also decided to try to bring to the attention of the novel's teachers the rich array of other texts (fictive, nonfictive, and musical) that influenced Ellison as well as the growing body of critical work about not only *Invisible Man* but also Ellison's other fiction and his essays. Our governing principle in introducing these other texts was whether they might enhance the teaching of the novel. Thus, in the "Materials" section, Pancho Savery discusses the secondary and primary sources that teachers have found useful for themselves and their students. He also highlights many of the literary, political, psychological, and historical works that illuminate aspects of the novel. In my introduction on the "Approaches" section, I try to provide an overview of some of the thematic and pedagogical questions that the novel raises and that many of the volume's essays explore. And, of course, the essays themselves demonstrate the extraordinarily varied ways in which the novel can be taught. The volume concludes with sample study guides, a list of respondents to the survey and contributors to the volume, a bibliography of works cited, and an index.

There are many people to thank for their help in the preparation of this volume, most particularly our contributors, who through their admiration and regard for *Invisible Man* have taught us a good deal, and our students, who in their enthusiasm for and engagement in the novel seem always to reaffirm its significance and vitality. As one of my students recently wrote me, quoting the *Invisible Man*'s narrator, the novel "has illuminated the blackness of my invisibility" (13). Special thanks go to Maureen Modlish, my executive secretary, for typing this manuscript with an editor's eye; to my University of Tulsa colleagues Gordon Taylor, Norman S. Grabo, Denise Lardner Carmody, and Thomas F. Staley for encouraging me during some of the difficult moments in the book's evolution; to my staff in the College of Arts and Sciences Dean's Office for helping me find precious moments in which I could attend to the manuscript; to Phyllis Franklin, executive director of the MLA, and Joseph Gibaldi, general editor of the *Approaches* series, for caring about the project; and to my daughter Alexandra for teaching me—again and again—what really matters.

SRP

Part One

MATERIALS

Pancho Savery

Readings for Students

The length of *Invisible Man* and the limited amount of time instructors have to teach the novel make it virtually impossible to require much outside reading. Most assigned reading consists of background materials and essays from *Shadow and Act* and *Going to the Territory* rather than critical works about the novel. One respondent to the MLA survey of Ellison instructors says that reading secondary sources "doesn't satisfy the students or me." Another explains, "Because undergraduates have a good deal of difficulty learning to formulate their own responses to a work of literature, I prefer that they avoid critical reading. . . ." Typically, then, critical works are assigned only in advanced courses.

Many more teachers of *Invisible Man* recommend background or critical reading than require it. Indeed, most teachers suggest no outside reading of any kind. One survey response is typical: "Emphasis throughout is on the novel itself. . . . To go outside . . . when time is limited, can be a danger that robs the class of time needed for the novel itself." Another says, "Since this course already involves a substantial amount of reading, I try to incorporate the necessary background material in my lectures and comments." While this respondent does not assign essays from *Shadow and Act* and *Going to the Territory*, she quotes from them "rather extensively." Teachers concerned with Ellison's essays and interviews most often note "The Art of Fiction," "Harlem Is Nowhere," "The World and the Jug," "Hidden Name, Complex Fate," "A Very Stern Discipline," "Brave Words for a Startling Occasion," "Richard Wright's Blues," "Change the Joke and Slip the Yoke," and "On Bird, Bird-Watching, and Jazz" (all from *Shadow and Act*); "Portrait of Inman Page," "Society, Morality, and the Novel," "The Novel as a Function of American Democracy," "The Little Man at Chehaw Station," "Going to the Territory," "The Art of Romare Bearden," "On Initiation Rites and Power," "Remembering Richard Wright," and "Perspective of Literature" (from *Going to the Territory*); Ellison's introduction to the thirtieth anniversary edition of *Invisible Man*; the uncollected essays "Stormy Weather" and "The Uses of History in Fiction"; and the interviews with Geller; Cannon, Raphael, and Thompson; Reed, Troupe, and Cannon; Stepto and Harper; Hersey; O'Brien; McPherson; Forrest; and Girson.

Some respondents to the survey also described their need and that of their students to be informed about the historical, literary, philosophical, psychological, and political roots of the novel. Such information is included in "Background Materials for Teachers" later in this section.

The Instructor's Library

The survey of Ellison teachers shows that the novel is taught in a variety of courses. Most common, as would be expected, are survey courses in American and Afro-American literature, but respondents also teach the novel in such courses as Freshman Composition, Southern Literature, Introduction to Fiction, The Modern Novel, The Picaresque Mode, The 1950s, and Humanistic Perspectives.

What follows is a checklist of essential reference works and critical studies that the teacher of *Invisible Man* should ideally know. Indeed, survey respondents often identified them as essential. Since there is relatively little consensus about the best work on *Invisible Man* and since new articles appear each year, the list is necessarily incomplete. Instructors are therefore encouraged to keep up with such journals as *Black American Literature Forum*, *CLA Journal*, *Callaloo*, and *MELUS*. The yearly bibliographies of the MLA and *American Literature* and the annual bibliographical essays on Afro-American literature in *American Literary Scholarship* should also be consulted.

Reference

The only text in this category is Jacqueline Covo's 1974 volume *The Blinking Eye: Ralph Waldo Ellison and His American, French, German, and Italian Critics, 1952–1971*. It includes checklists of criticism and long bibliographic essays that are evaluative as well as descriptive. Leonard Deutsch updates the criticism through 1977 in his entry on Ellison in *American Novelists since World War II* (*Dictionary of Literary Biography*, vol. 2). For a complete list of Ellison's work to date, consult the bibliography in Robert O'Meally's *Craft of Ralph Ellison*.

Critical Studies

Book-Length Studies

At this writing, there are only two book-length studies of Ellison, Robert O'Meally's *Craft of Ralph Ellison* and Robert List's *Dedalus in Harlem: The Joyce-Ellison Connection*. List's work has many limitations. The chapters have no titles, there is no bibliography, and there is no mention of O'Meally's volume. List often makes it seem as though Ellison merely copied Joyce's themes and techniques, and List's Freudian reading is reductive. He fails to ground his analysis in the Afro-American tradition. (Houston Baker's analysis of Trueblood [*Blues* 172–99], which also uses Freud, is a model for what is missing in List.) List is also inattentive to detail. For example, he twice identifies "Oh They Picked Poor Robin Clean" as a composition by Charlie Parker, when Ellison, in *Shadow and Act*, clearly assigns it to the Blue Devils Orchestra during the thirties.

O'Meally's book, by contrast, is the best overall treatment to date on Ellison's work. O'Meally provides ample biographical material on Ellison's life in Oklahoma, his experiences at Tuskegee, and his early years "up North." He also offers detailed analyses of Ellison's relationship with Richard Wright, his early short stories, his publications since *Invisible Man*, his aesthetic theories, and his influence on younger writers. The center of the book is O'Meally's chapter on *Invisible Man*, "Invisible Man: Black and Blue." His theses are that folklore "is a key to Ellison's fictional world," that Ellison "links the central question of identity to that of history and folklore" (2), and that even Ellison's "most apt critics" have treated this aspect of the novel "fleetingly" (78). Although O'Meally does not fully explore all aspects of Ellison's use of folklore, his work is groundbreaking and should be the starting point for all future studies of Ellison. In particular, his book is useful in identifying Afro-American folk patterns such as underground trails, the razzings of the black yokel, the running motif, the role of the dog, black sermonic devices, and the characteristics of the blues, spirituals, signifying, and the dozens. He also conveniently identifies various pieces of music played by artists such as Count Basie, Billy Eckstine, Earl "Fatha" Hines, Jimmy Rushing, and Bessie Smith, providing essential information for those who wish to use music in their teaching. Along with *Shadow and Act*, *Going to the Territory*, and the collections of essays by Reilly, Hersey, and Benston, O'Meally's book is the most often cited essential source for both students and teachers of *Invisible Man*.

Collections of Essays

In addition to the three journal issues devoted to Ellison (*CLA Journal* 13, 1970; *Black World* 20, 1970; and *Carleton Miscellany* 18, 1980), there are five collections of essays devoted to *Invisible Man*: John Reilly's *Twentieth Century Interpretations of* Invisible Man, Ronald Gottesman's *The Merrill Studies in* Invisible Man, Joseph Trimmer's *Casebook on Ralph Ellison's* Invisible Man, John Hersey's *Ralph Ellison: A Collection of Critical Essays*, a volume in the Twentieth Century Views series, and Kimberly Benston's *Speaking for You: The Vision of Ralph Ellison*. Reilly's, Hersey's, and Benston's collections are the easiest to obtain. Unfortunately, despite the many excellent articles on *Invisible Man*, there is unnecessary repetition. For example, when Trimmer's book was published, six of its nine critical essays had already appeared in Reilly or Gottesman, and five of Hersey's selections had already appeared in Reilly, Gottesman, or Trimmer. Robert Bone's "Ralph Ellison and the Uses of the Imagination" appears in four of the collections, and both William Schafer's "Ralph Ellison and the Birth of the Anti-Hero" and Earl Rovit's "Ralph Ellison and the American Comic Tradition" appear in three of the five collections. Trimmer's volume, however, unlike the other four, also contains an excellent selection of background essays that is particularly valuable for students.

Reilly's collection contains fifteen pieces, including early reviews by Lloyd L. Brown from *Masses and Mainstream* and Anthony West from the *New Yorker*. The ten major essays generally fall into two categories: analyses of theme, structure, or symbol and attempts to place Ellison in a tradition. In the first category are M. K. Singleton, "Leadership Mirages as Antagonists in *Invisible Man*"; William J. Schafer, "Irony from Underground—Satiric Elements in *Invisible Man*"; Charles I. Glicksberg, "The Symbolism of Vision"; Selma Fraiberg, "Two Modern Incest Heroes"; and Ellin Horowitz, "The Rebirth of the Artist." Therman B. O'Daniel provides a general overview of the novel and of some of its critics in "The Image of Man as Portrayed by Ralph Ellison." Attempts to place the novel in a tradition are provided by Earl H. Rovit, "Ralph Ellison and the American Comic Tradition," and Esther Merle Jackson, "The American Negro and the Image of the Absurd." The two essays in this collection most often mentioned by survey respondents as essential are Robert Bone's "Ralph Ellison and the Uses of the Imagination" and Floyd R. Horowitz's "Ralph Ellison's Modern Version of Brer Bear and Brer Rabbit in *Invisible Man*." These essays are important for their uses of Afro-American music and folklore as bases of analysis, areas that would be further explored in the explosion of Ellison criticism in the 1970s.

Ronald Gottesman's volume contains only eight essays and, unlike Reilly's volume, lacks a chronology, a bibliography, and a significant introduction by the editor. This collection also duplicates three of Reilly's selections: the essays by Bone and Floyd Horowitz and the reprint of "The Art of Fiction" from *Shadow and Act*. The other essays are Marcus Klein's "Ralph Ellison's *Invisible Man*," which provides a general overview but concludes that the novel "doesn't finally go anywhere"; Steven Marcus's "American Negro in Search of Identity," which is mostly about James Baldwin; Thomas Vogler's general overview "*Invisible Man*: Somebody's Protest Novel"; William J. Schafer's "Ralph Ellison and the Birth of the Anti-Hero"; and Stewart Rodnon's "Ralph Ellison's *Invisible Man*: Six Tentative Approaches."

From the student perspective, Trimmer's collection is perhaps the best. The first half of the book, entitled "The Historical Tradition," contains essential background essays for students on the "racial heritage" and the "artistic heritage." The first section includes Booker T. Washington, "Atlanta Exposition Address"; W. E. B. Du Bois, "Of Mr. Booker T. Washington and Others"; Alain Locke, "The New Negro"; Marcus Garvey, "An Appeal to the Conscience of the Black Race to See Itself"; and Richard Wright, "I Tried to Be a Communist." The section on the artistic heritage includes Ralph Waldo Emerson, "The Poet"; T. S. Eliot, "Tradition and the Individual Talent"; Sterling Brown, "Negro Character as Seen by White Authors"; and Irving Howe, "Black Boys and Native Sons." The second half of the book contains two essays from *Shadow and Act*, "The World and the Jug" and "Brave Words for a Startling Occasion," and eight critical essays. Of the eight, essays by Robert Bone, Floyd Horowitz, Ellin Horowitz, and Earl Rovit are repetitions from Reilly, and William Schafer's is a repeat from Gottesman. The three remaining essays are Alice Bloch's "Sight Imagery in *Invisible Man*"; Marvin E. Mangelin's "Whitman and Ellison: Older Symbols in a Modern Mainstream," which compares Homer Barbee's sermon to Whitman's "When Lilacs Last in the Dooryard Bloom'd"; and Richard Kostelanetz's "Politics of Ellison's Booker: *Invisible Man* as Symbolic History."

Like Reilly's collection, John Hersey's contains a selection of short reviews as well as longer critical essays. There are reviews of both *Invisible Man* (by Saul Bellow) and *Shadow and Act* (by Robert Penn Warren, Lawrence Washington Chisolm, and Stanley Edgar Hyman), as well as the Ellison section of Irving Howe's "Black Boys and Native Sons." Of the eight critical essays, those by Bone and Rovit are repeats from Reilly, and those by Schafer and Vogler repeats from Gottesman. In "Violence in Afro-American Fiction: An Hypothesis" Stephen B. Bennett and William W. Nichols suggest that "apocalyptic rage" is at the heart of much Afro-American fiction, and in "The Music of Invisibility" Tony Tanner provides a general overview of what he calls "the most profound novel about American identity written since the war." The two remaining essays, George E. Kent's "Ralph Ellison and the Afro-American Folk and Cultural Tradition" and Larry Neal's "Ellison's Zoot Suit," are among the most important essays written on *Invisible Man*. More than anyone before them, Kent and Neal ground their work in the Afro-American folk tradition and demonstrate its fundamental importance in understanding and analyzing Ellison's novel. Hersey's volume also includes two other selections, James Alan McPherson's profile-interview "Indivisible Man" and John Hersey's new interview with Ellison, "A Completion of Personality."

The most recent collection is Kimberly Benston's *Speaking for You: The Vision of Ralph Ellison*. Not only does this volume contain almost no essays that have already appeared in the previous collections, since most were commissioned especially for this volume or were previously uncollected, but Benston wanted essays with a particular point of view. As he notes in his introduction:

> . . . I found that the criticism tended to collect at either of two extremes: descriptive-aesthetic and prescriptive-ideological. This volume

reflects an effort to redress this schism by suggesting an image of a more complex and coherent career.

The essays in this collection have been chosen and organized to reflect the dynamic *interplay* of aesthetic practice and cultural perception which I take to be the cornerstone of Ellison's vision. Indeed nothing unites the essays gathered here more than the collective intuition of Ellison's central "moral" ideal: the dialectical mutuality of conscience and craft that enables the artist to dare "speak for you." (7–8)

Included are essays by Charles Davis, Houston Baker, Wilson Harris, Hortense Spillers, Claudia Tate, Michel Fabre, Leon Forrest, and Kenneth Burke.

Uncollected Essays

A larger number of essays on Ellison, published before and since the five collections appeared remain uncollected, making it virtually impossible for teachers to have read them all. The partial listing that follows includes works cited in responses to the survey as well as works thought significant by the editors but not mentioned by teachers.

Among general overviews and thematic studies of the novel are Houston A. Baker, Jr., *The Journey Back*; Jonathan Baumbach, "Nightmare of a Native Son: Ellison's *Invisible Man*"; C. W. E. Bigsby, "From Protest to Paradox: The Black Writer at Mid Century"; Robert Bone, *The Negro Novel in America*; Lloyd W. Brown, "Black Entitles: Names as Symbols in Afro-American Literature"; John Callahan, "The Historical Frequencies of Ralph Ellison" and "Democracy and the Pursuit of Narrative"; Barbara Christian, "Ralph Ellison: A Critical Study"; John Henrik Clarke, "The Visible Dimension of *Invisible Man*"; Eugenia W. Collier, "The Nightmare Truth of an Invisible Man"; Michael G. Cooke, *Afro-American Literature in the Twentieth Century: The Achievement of Intimacy*; Arthur P. Davis, *From the Dark Tower*; Russell G. Fischer, "*Invisible Man* as History"; Nick Aaron Ford, "The Ambivalence of Ralph Ellison"; Leon Forrest, "Racial History as a Clue to the Action in *Invisible Man*"; Edward M. Griffin, "Notes from a Clean, Well-Lighted Place: Ralph Ellison's *Invisible Man*"; Vincent Harding, "Black Reflections on the Cultural Ramifications of Black Identity"; Ihab Hassan, *Radical Innocence: Studies in the Contemporary American Novel*; J. N. Heermance, "A White Critic's Viewpoint: The Modern Negro Novel"; Abby Arthur Johnson, "Birds of Passage: Flight Imagery in *Invisible Man*"; Alfred Kazin, *Bright Book of Life*; E. M. Kirst, "A Langian Analysis of Blackness in Ralph Ellison's *Invisible Man*"; Phyllis R. Klotman, "The Running Man as Metaphor in Ellison's *Invisible Man*"; R. W. Nash, "Stereotypes and Social Types in Ellison's *Invisible Man*"; Carolyn Sylvander, "Ralph Ellison's *Invisible Man* and Female Stereotypes"; Darwin T. Turner, "Sight in *Invisible Man*"; and Eleanor R. Wilner, "The Invisible Black Thread: Identity and Nonentity in *Invisible Man*."

A number of structural studies and articles compare Ellison to other writers. As the following list demonstrates, the possibilities are wide, and good work continues to be done. Among these are Michael Allen, "Some Examples of Faulknerian Rhetoric in Ellison's *Invisible Man*"; Houston A. Baker, Jr., "A Forgotten Prototype: *The Autobiography of an Ex-Colored Man* and *Invisible Man*"; Kimberly Benston, "Ellison, Baraka, and the Faces of Tradition"; Lloyd W. Brown, "Ralph Ellison's Exhorters: The Role of Rhetoric in *Invisible Man*"; Jerry H. Bryant, "Wright, Ellison, Baldwin: Exorcising the Demon"; Robert J. Butler, "Dante's *Inferno* and Ellison's *Invisible Man*: A Study in Literary Continuity"; Eugenia Collier, "Dimensions of Alienation in Two Black American and Caribbean Novels"; Leonard J. Deutsch, "Ralph Waldo Ellison and Ralph Waldo Emerson: A Shared Moral Vision" and "*The Waste Land* in Ellison's *Invisible Man*"; Barbara Fass, "Rejection of Paternalism: Hawthorne's 'My Kinsman Major Molineux' and Ellison's *Invisible Man*"; Robert Fleming, "Contemporary Themes in Johnson's *Autobiography of an Ex-Colored Man*"; Joseph Frank, "Ralph Ellison and a Literary 'Ancestor': Dostoevsky"; Donald B. Gibson, "Ralph Ellison and James Baldwin"; William Goede, "On Lower Frequencies: The Buried Men in Wright and Ellison"; Marcia R. Lieberman, "Moral Innocents: Ellison's *Invisible Man* and *Candide*"; Robert O'Meally, "The Rules of Magic: Hemingway as Ellison's 'Ancestor' "; Stewart Rodnon, "*The Adventures of Huckleberry Finn* and *Invisible Man*: Thematic and Structural Comparisons" and "Henry Adams and Ralph Ellison: Transcending Tragedy"; Archie D. Sanders, "Odysseus in Black: An Analysis of the Structure of *Invisible Man*"; Elizabeth A. Schultz, "The Heirs of Ralph Ellison: Patterns of Individualism in the Contemporary Afro-American Novel"; Joseph T. Skerrett, "The Wright Interpretation: Ralph Ellison and the Anxiety of Influence"; Nancy M. Tischler, "Negro Literature and Classic Form"; John Vassilowitch, Jr., "Ellison's Dr. Bledsoe: Two Literary Sources"; Mary Ellen Williams Walsh, "*Invisible Man*: Ralph Ellison's Wasteland"; and Phillip Williams, "A Comparative Approach to Afro-American and Neo-African Novels: Ellison and Achebe."

Of particular note as structural analyses are Robert B. Stepto's *From behind the Veil: A Study of Afro-American Narrative* and Henry Louis Gates, Jr.'s "Blackness of Blackness: A Critique of the Sign and the Signifying Monkey."

Although not the most productive numerically, the area of folk culture has generated the most significant growth in Ellison studies. Larry Neal's "Ellison's Zoot Suit" is a landmark piece in this field, not only because it is critically brilliant, but because it signals a rapproachment between Black Aestheticians and Ellison. (For a history of the change in attitude toward Ellison by both Larry Neal and Stephen Henderson, as well as a critique of the work of Stepto and Gates, see Houston Baker, "Discovering America: Generational Shifts, Afro-American Literary Criticism, and the Study of Expressive Culture," in his *Blues, Ideology, and Afro-American Literature: A Vernacular Theory*, and his "Critical Change and Blues Continuity: An Essay on the Criticism of Larry Neal.")

Nineteen-seventy also marked the publication of Albert Murray's *Omni-Americans*. In the chapters "The Blues Idiom and the Mainstream" and "James Baldwin, Protest Fiction, and the Blues Tradition," Murray analyzes the blues idiom as a complex, life-affirming, existential art form and convincingly argues that *Invisible Man* is "par excellence the literary extension of the blues." All Murray's works—*The Hero and the Blues, Stomping the Blues, South to a Very Old Place, Train Whistle Guitar*—are valuable. Murray and Ellison on the blues should be read in conjunction with Baraka's *Blues People*. While Murray and Ellison see the blues as primarily artistic and totally American, Baraka sees African elements in the blues and has a much more political outlook. Other important work in the field of Ellison and folk culture includes Susan L. Blake, "Ritual and Rationalization: Black Folklore in the Works of Ralph Ellison"; Gene Bluestein, *The Voice of the Folk*; Joseph Boskin, "The Life and Death of Sambo: Overview of an Historical Hang-up"; Lawrence J. Clipper, "Folkloric and Mythic Elements in *Invisible Man*"; Trudier Harris, "Ellison's 'Peter Wheatstraw': His Basis in Black Folk Tradition"; Stanley Edgar Hyman, *The Promised End*; and Robert O'Meally, "Riffs and Rituals: Folklore in the Work of Ralph Ellison."

Finally, Houston Baker's *Blues, Ideology, and Afro-American Literature: A Vernacular Theory*, represents a new direction in Afro-American literary criticism. Baker finds a "blues matrix" at the center of Afro-American culture that is rooted in the vernacular. In addition, he goes beyond previous commentators on the blues by attempting to forge a synthesis between the Black Aestheticians with their romantic, Marxist emphasis on content (Henderson and Neal) and those he calls "reconstructionists," who are overconcerned with form (Gates and Stepto). Baker acknowledges debts to both sides and goes beyond them by devoting attention to the economics of the blues. His analysis culminates in "To Move without Moving: Creativity and Commerce in Ralph Ellison's Trueblood Episode."

Background Studies

Among general histories, the two most often mentioned are John Hope Franklin, *From Slavery to Freedom*, and J. Saunders Redding, *They Came in Chains.* Together, the works cover the entire history of Afro-Americans, from 4000 BC to well into the twentieth century, and both have been revised since their initial publications in 1947 and 1950, respectively. Although it covers a much shorter period of time, *Harlem Renaissance* by Nathan Irvin Huggins provides both a literary and a historical background to the period immediately preceding that in which Ellison seriously turned his attention to writing. Perhaps even better than Huggins's book is David Levering Lewis's *When Harlem Was in Vogue.* It covers the same time span as Huggins does but provides a better social history. Amiri Baraka's *Blues People* successfully combines history, music, sociology, and politics. Despite Ellison's quarrels with Baraka, *Blues People* remains a classic study that many survey respondents recommend.

For background on black life, respondents recommended James Baldwin, *Notes of a Native Son*; Claude Brown, *Manchild in the Promised Land*; Eldridge Cleaver, *Soul on Ice*; Frantz Fanon, *The Wretched of the Earth*; Malcolm X, *The Autobiography of Malcolm X*; John Howard Griffin, *Black like Me*; and Albert Murray, *The Omni-Americans.*

Communism and Marxism

Mark Naison's *Communists in Harlem during the Depression* is the basic text on the role of blacks in the American Communist movement. Written from a more personal perspective, but also very valuable, is Harold Cruse's *Crisis of the Negro Intellectual.* Roi Ottley's *New World A-Coming* is a study of blacks in Harlem that gives attention to this topic, and Angelo Herndon's autobiography, *Let Me Live*, is the story of a black Communist. Also essential on this topic is Richard Wright's *American Hunger*, originally a part of *Black Boy.* An excerpt is printed in Richard Crossman's *The God Who Failed*, which also includes essays by André Gide, Arthur Koestler, Ignazio Silone, Louis Fischer, and Stephen Spender about their disillusionment with communism.

On the Marxist view of history, Marx's *Economic and Philosophic Manuscripts of 1844*, *The German Ideology*, and the preface to *A Contribution to the Critique of Political Economy*, as well as Engels's *Socialism: Utopian and Scientific*, are probably the best works. Robert C. Tucker's *Marx-Engels Reader* prints large sections of all these. On the relationship between the party and the masses, Lenin's *What Is to Be Done (Essential Works)* and Appignanesi and Zarate's *Lenin for Beginners* are the most useful places to start. Gramsci's "Formation of the Intellectuals" in *Prison Notebooks* presents the opposite view from that of Lenin. In the play *Occupations* Trevor Griffiths contrasts what he calls "Leninist principle" and the "Gramscian principle."

Freud

Calvin S. Hall's *Primer of Freudian Psychology* is a short useful introduction to Freud's ideas and terminology. It is particularly clear on the distinction between ego, id, and superego, which informs the scene with Supercargo and the vets at the Golden Day. Freud's *Totem and Taboo* (which the invisible man sees in young Emerson's office), along with Patrick Mullahy, *Oedipus: Myth and Complex*, and Henri F. Ellenberger, *The Discovery of the Unconscious*, explains Freudian ideas on the banishment of growing sons, the sons' eventual slaying and eating of their fathers, their subsequent guilt, and their abstinence from sex with women. Erik Erikson's *Identity: Youth and Crisis* is also valuable.

Key Afro-American Historical Figures

References abound in the novel to Frederick Douglass, Booker T. Washington, W. E. B. Du Bois, Marcus Garvey, and Ras Tafari. Appropriate background reading is readily available. The best sources of information on Douglass are his three autobiographies: *Narrative of the Life of Frederick Douglass, an American Slave, Written by Himself* (1845); *My Bondage and My Freedom* (1855); and *The Life and Times of Frederick Douglass* (1881). Nathan Huggins provides an excellent introduction to Douglass's life and thought in *Slave and Citizen: The Life of Frederick Douglass*.

Booker T. Washington is an especially important presence in the novel. In his high school graduation speech, the invisible man quotes Washington's 1895 Atlanta Exposition Address, which is the fourteenth chapter of *Up from Slavery*, Washington's autobiography. *Up from Slavery*, W. E. B. Du Bois's *Souls of Black Folk* (in which Du Bois challenges Washington in "Of Mr. Booker T. Washington and Others"), and James Weldon Johnson's *Autobiography of An Ex-Colored Man* are also important literary sources for *Invisible Man* and comprise *Three Negro Classics*, edited by John Hope Franklin. Francis L. Broderick, *W. E. B. DuBois: Negro Leader in a Time of Crisis*, and Arnold Rampersad, *The Art and Imagination of W. E. B. Dubois*, are the standard texts with which to begin to understand Du Bois's life and work.

Ras Tafari (Haile Selassie, emperor of Ethiopia) is reflected in Ellison's Ras, who is also associated with Marcus Garvey. In a speech delivered at Liberty Hall in New York in August 1921, Garvey said, "At this moment methinks I see Ethiopia stretching forth her hands unto God, and methinks I see the Angel of God taking up the standard of the Red, the Black and the Green, and saying 'Men of the Negro Race, Men of Ethiopia, follow me' " (1: 96). The modern Rastafarians take their name from the emperor they saw as the incarnation of God, and they consider Garvey's greatness surpassed only by that of Haile Selassie. For information on Garvey, consult his *Philosophy and Opinions of Marcus Garvey* and also John Henrik Clarke's *Marcus Garvey and the Vision of Africa*, E. David Cronon's *Black Moses: The Story of Marcus Garvey and the Universal Negro Improvement Association*, and Amy Jacques-Garvey's *Garvey and Garveyism*. Because Rastafarianism, in addition to being a philosophy, is also at the heart of reggae music, the work of reggae musicians is a particularly rich field to mine. Foremost among these musicians was Bob Marley, whose albums are crucial to an understanding of Rastafarianism. Useful texts include Leonard Barrett, *The Rastafarians: Sounds of Cultural Dissonance*; Adrian Boot and Vivien Goldman, *Bob Marley: Soul Rebel–Natural Mystic*; Stephen Davis and Peter Simon, *Reggae Bloodlines* and *Reggae International*; Stephen Davis, *Bob Marley*; Millard Faristzaddi, *Itations of Jamaica and I Rastafari*; Tracy Nicholas and Bill Sparrow, *Rastafari: A Way of Life*; and Timothy White, *Catch a Fire: The Life of Bob Marley*.

American Culture

Although this is a category for which most teachers in the survey did not have suggestions, three titles were prominently mentioned: R. W. B. Lewis, *The American Adam*; Alexis de Tocqueville, *Democracy in America*; and Ernest Tuveson, *Redeemer Nation*.

The Literary Tradition

The list of works that Ellison alludes to as well as of the authors he cites as influences is long. Many are mentioned in "The Instructor's Library" under "Uncollected Essays." Teachers of the novel found the following literary works important: Fyodor Dostoevsky, *Notes from Underground*; W. E. B. Du Bois, *The Souls of Black Folk*; T. S. Eliot, *The Waste Land*; Ralph Waldo Emerson, "Self-Reliance" and "The American Scholar"; Zora Neale Hurston, *Their Eyes Were Watching God*; James Weldon Johnson, *The Autobiography of an Ex-Colored Man*; James Joyce, *A Portrait of the Artist as a Young Man*; Herman Melville, *Moby-Dick*, *Benito Cereno*, and *The Confidence Man*; J. Saunders Redding, *No Day of Triumph* and *Stranger and Alone*; Mark Twain, *The Adventures of Huckleberry Finn*; Booker T. Washington, *Up from Slavery*; H. G. Wells, *The Invisible Man*; Walt Whitman, "Song of Myself," "Calamus," and "Memories of President Lincoln"; and Richard Wright, "The Man Who Lived Underground," *Native Son*, and *Black Boy*.

It is interesting to compare this last group with Ellison's own list. Prior to a panel on his work at the 1983 MLA convention in New York, Ellison told us that the five essential background works to read are Melville's *Moby-Dick*, Malraux's *Man's Fate*, Stendhal's *Red and the Black*, Twain's *Huckleberry Finn*, and Dostoevsky's *Brothers Karamazov*.

Existentialism

Regarding the many versions and definitions of existentialism, Ellison has been explicit about what he likes and doesn't like. Philosophical and literary antecedents include Kierkegaard, Nietzsche, Heidegger, Dostoevsky, Unamuno, Malraux, Sartre, and Camus. Walter Kaufmann's *Existentialism from Dostoevsky to Sartre* and William V. Spanos's *Casebook on Existentialism* collect many important primary sources. Although Ellison's existentialism derives more from Unamuno and Malraux than from Camus and Sartre, Sartre's "Existentialism" (in both collections; entitled "Existentialism Is a Humanism" in Kaufmann) is a key document and provides an excellent introduction for students. Other studies include William Barrett, *Irrational Man* and *Time of Need*; Ernst Breisach, *Introduction to Modern Existentialism*; and Germaine Brée, *Camus and Sartre*. Among literary works that influenced Ellison are Unamuno, "Saint Manuel Bueno, Martyr," *The Tragic Sense of Life in Men and Nations*, *The Agony of Christianity*, and *Our Lord Don Quixote*; and Malraux, *Man's Fate*, *Man's Hope*, *Days of Wrath*, and *The Voices of Silence*.

Music

As with assigning outside reading, most teachers feel there isn't enough time to play in class the various musical pieces Ellison refers to, including Louis Armstrong's version of "Black and Blue." Nevertheless, teachers should be aware of the many musical references in order to make use of them if they choose.

My essay in part 2 identifies most of the blues pieces in the novel, and Robert O'Meally's book identifies other pieces. The novel also mentions music that is not Afro-American, such as Beethoven's Fifth Symphony and Dvořák's Ninth Symphony (*From the New World*). Ellison, it should be remembered, wanted to be a composer, and music can help teachers illuminate some of the novel's key formal and thematic aspects.

Part Two

APPROACHES

INTRODUCTION
Susan Resneck Parr

When the narrator-protagonist of *Invisible Man*, in the dream sequence in the prologue, announces, "I too have become acquainted with ambivalence" (10), he is calling attention to one of the novel's major themes: that, as he concludes in the epilogue, he will "denounce and defend, . . . condemn and affirm, say no and say yes, say yes and say no," and love as well as hate (566–67). The object of a good deal of his ambivalence is no less than an American society that does not recognize his humanity and the humanity of other blacks. The forms his ambivalence takes are, on the one hand, to denounce, condemn, and say no to those institutions and those people— white and black alike—who will not see him and, on the other hand, to defend, affirm, and say yes to the democratic principles on which the United States was founded.

In fact, the invisible man goes another step and uses that ambivalence as a basis for his personal (existential) philosophy. Committing himself to action that will be socially responsible, he nevertheless insists that whatever choices he makes, whatever "plan of living" he selects for himself, he "must never lose sight of the chaos against which that pattern was conceived" (567). He also concludes that "[l]ife is to be lived, not controlled; and humanity is won by continuing to play in the face of certain defeat" (564). Accepting the notion that visibility lies in the eye of the beholder, he determines that even if unseen, he will see. As he puts it, "I'm invisible, not blind" (563). In other words, he comes to embrace consciousness and possibility even as he rejects any specific plan of action other than that of telling his tale, an act about which he also feels ambivalence:

> Here I've set out to throw my anger into the world's face, but now that I've tried to put it all down the old fascination with playing a role returns, and I'm drawn upward again. So that even before I finish I've failed (maybe my anger is too heavy; perhaps, being a talker, I've used too many words). But I've failed. The very act of trying to put it all down has confused me and negated some of the anger and some of the bitterness.   (566)

But he will also put that ambivalence aside in order to end his hibernation and to try—as Louis Armstrong did—"to make music of invisibility" (14).

There is nothing ambivalent, however, about Ellison's grounding of the novel in the black American experience, especially in the folklore that Robert G. O'Meally identifies in his *Craft of Ralph Ellison* as "an index to the Afro-American and thus to the general American past" and as "a key to Ellison's fictional world." As O'Meally demonstrates, Ellison is indebted to "sermons, tales, games, jokes, boasts, toasts, dozens, blues, spirituals" (2). Moreover, on its most immediate level, the novel can be read as an account of the various options available to a young black man in America from the time after Reconstruction to the present of the novel. For example, at various moments in the novel the invisible man either encounters or tries to emulate blacks who with varying motives, sometimes self-serving, play the role of a so-called Uncle Tom. At other moments he aspires to be like Frederick Douglass, Booker T. Washington, and Marcus Garvey. He also comes for a time to believe that the solution to racial injustice is with the American Communist party (the Brotherhood), and he is momentarily attracted to violence. He also sees as an option the fictional Rinehart, who, concerned only with his own profit, entertains no thoughts of social and political revolutions but instead is a runner, a gambler, a briber, a lover, and a preacher.

At the same time, however, Ellison deliberately universalizes the invisible man's experience through literary allusions, the novel's structure, and direct statements. Young Emerson tells the invisible man, "With us it's still Jim and Huck Finn" (184), invites him to the Club Calamus (182), and keeps a copy of *Totem and Taboo* on his coffee table (177), all references that invite the reader to think about the novel in terms of Emerson, Whitman, Twain, and Freud. The presence of the blind Homer Barbee reinforces the sense that the invisible man is embarked on an odyssey of his own toward sight and insight. The frequent references to snakes that appear as the invisible man is being expelled from or choosing to leave what he falsely believed to be Edenic situations (e.g., 21, 154, 266, 374, and 568), his opening a Bible to Genesis but failing to read it (159), and his encounter on the subway with a blonde girl eating a red Delicious apple (244)—all underscore the novel's concern with losing innocence and gaining the knowledge of good and evil. Further universalizing the novel are the scene with Supercargo, based on a series of puns grounded in Freud's notion of the id, the ego, and the superego; the recurrent oedipal motifs (both Freudian and Sophoclean versions) that are manifest in the invisible man's search for a rejection of various false father figures; and the direct references to Joyce's *Portrait of the Artist as a Young Man*, Conrad's *Heart of Darkness*, Dostoevsky's *Notes from Underground*, Wright's "Man Who Lived Underground," Eliot's *Waste Land*, the Marxist notion of history, Dvořák's *New World* Symphony, and a host of other works. And, of course, the novel's last line, "Who knows but that, on the lower frequencies, I speak for you?" (568) overtly asserts Ellison's use of the black American experience as a metaphor for the human condition.

These two aspects of the novel—the narrator's failure to unhesitatingly embrace a particular course of social action and to advocate a particular political point of view, on the one hand, and the novel's indebtedness to both black American and Western culture, on the other hand—have led to certain critical ambivalences about the work. In 1963 Irving Howe criticized Ellison (and James Baldwin) for not emulating Richard Wright's *Native Son* and writing protest novels. In 1971 Addison Gayle, Jr., articulating his concept of the "Black Aesthetic," insisted that *Invisible Man* was flawed because it was "wedded to the concept of assimilation at a time when such a concept has ceased to be the preoccupation of the black writer" (392). Robert O'Meally, in contrast, concluded that Ellison's importance lay "in his unsinkable optimism concerning his race, his nation, man's fate" and "in his insistence on literary craft under the pressure of inspiration as the best means of transforming everyday experience, talk and lore into literature" (*Craft* 181).

The question of whether to approach the novel in social and political terms or in literary terms is apparent in the essays in this volume. Although all sixteen contributors appear to be in accord with James Walton, who insists to his students that Ellison deserves artistic freedom, they offer differing opinions about which aspect of the novel is most deserving of emphasis. Some argue that a thematic approach is the most appropriate because the text can and should speak for itself. Others are as fervent that the novel cannot be understood unless its readers are informed about the literary, biblical, psychological, musical, philosophical, classical, and historical motifs that permeate it. The question, of course, can be put more crudely: Should class time emphasize the invisible man's search for self, or should it be devoted to the symbolic texture of the novel (e.g., to the images of blindness and sight, invisibility and visibility, father figures, snakes, black Sambo figures, documents that can't be shed, and colors)? Is it enough for students to think about such characters as Bledsoe and Ras as Ellison presents them, or should they also know about Booker T. Washington, Marcus Garvey, and the Rastafarians? How useful is it for students to listen to Louis Armstrong's "Black and Blue" and Dvořák's *New World* Symphony with its mixture of classical, folk, and spiritual strains? Do they need to know about Freud to understand what the veteran doctor means when he tells the invisible man to be his own father? Should they also be asked to read Ellison's interviews and his brilliant essays about music, literature, and social issues in *Shadow and Act* and *Going to the Territory*?

On some level, all these questions find resolution in the teaching of the novel. As the essays to follow indicate, the shape of the course, the level of students, the time allotted to the novel, and the instructor's beliefs about what is most significant dictate the ways teachers present *Invisible Man* to their students. In selecting the essays to be included in this volume, we have therefore embraced, as the narrator does, the principle of diversity, of pluralism. Indeed, we have tried to heed the novel's warning about the distortion that comes from imposing one pattern on whatever reality one perceives and the dangers of trying to "stick to the plan" (172). Moreover, although we and our contributors recognize that in its richness, the novel eludes full explication and definitive readings, we—like the invisible man himself—hope to provide a beginning.

In the first two essays in the section "The Student and Teacher as Readers," James E. Walton and Walter Slatoff describe how they teach the novel to students who come to their classes with very different preconceptions about what literature should be. Walton, for instance, notes that his students, particularly his black students, are unhappy that *Invisible Man* leaves "unresolved many of the critical social and political issues it has so dramatically raised." Walton therefore tries to persuade his students that "Ellison, like all other artists, needs the freedom simply to develop his art—without making the obligatory 'dues-paying' statement" of writing protest literature. As Walton explains, "What I am arguing against, of course, is a tendency toward a monolithic approach to viewing literature by American black writers." Slatoff, by contrast, hopes that his students will be troubled by the novel and not see it primarily as "a great piece of literature." He himself has always found *Invisible Man* a particularly difficult book to talk about. "I've never been able to get much distance from it," he says. "It is as if I were reading a book about a war while still in the middle of that war." But even as he believes such lack of distance is "a good thing," Slatoff shows how the failure to create distance both for characters within the novel and for people in general can bring about personal torment and even threaten one's sanity.

John M. Reilly and Gordon O. Taylor argue for approaches that embrace both the political and the aesthetic. In an effort to bring students to see that *Invisible Man* is neither autobiographical nor merely a reflection of "the findings of sociology and history," Reilly encourages them to consider "Ellison's conception of self and life" and his use of his fictional persona as "Ellison's imaginative means of presenting American life" with all the contradictions inherent in American democracy. Reilly then leads his students to understand that both *Invisible Man* and *Shadow and Act* "represent personae acknowledging bitter experience but transcending it by affirming the power to control one's own destiny." Like Walton, Reilly wants his students to understand "the capacity of deliberate art to found a zone of freedom," something Reilly thinks of as "a principle of Afro-American life." Taylor too takes as his subject the tension between "literary and the social issues, between matters of aesthetic effect and matters of moral consequence." Illuminating the complex relationship between novelist and narrator (and reader) and the "gap" in the novel between "aesthetic composure on the one hand, and the volatility of personal completion on the other," Taylor sees such tension as "the field of force from which the act of Ellison's art proceeds." As he places the novel in a wide context of American and Afro-American fiction, Taylor also explores the ways in which "author, protagonist, and reader of *Invisible Man* alike, teacher and student together as well, are at once trapped and deliberately positioned in the space between reality and illusion, each of which appears in both benign and malignant aspects."

In the essay concluding this section, R. Baxter Miller enters this controversy by arguing that the reader must challenge the validity of both the invisible man's narrative voice and Ellison's authorial stance, which Miller considers self-deceived. Moreover, while Miller acknowledges *Invisible Man* as an "American masterpiece" and "a structural achievement in Euramerican literacy," he believes that in such achievements, Ellison has failed to "demand the imprint of [his] own fiction on American history." Miller's sometimes ideological presentation of Ellison and some of Ellison's critics may provoke controversy of its own.

The rest of the essays are divided into two sections. The first, "The Novel and Its Afro-American, American, and European Traditions," illustrates Miller's point about Ellison's indebtedness to the Euramerican tradition. The final section is "Teaching the Novel Thematically." The categories, of course, are not mutually exclusive, since all the essays in the first two sections focus on thematic concerns as well as on Ellison's influences.

Wilson J. Moses clearly identifies the difficulties of trying to separate out Ellison's "intellectual debts," of trying to understand the novel either solely as part of a self-contained Afro-American tradition or as totally outside that tradition. Thus Moses chides Ellison for "an unnecessary repudiation" of his debt to a black literary tradition even as Moses celebrates Ellison's desire to avoid "the reduction of his art to a system of stereotypes and clichés that pass for folklore." Pancho Savery too locates the invisible man's "search for his identity" both in Ellison's debt to the invisible man's folk past, especially to the blues, on the one hand, and to European existentialism, on the other. Savery argues that for Ellison the blues serve to "transcend the pain of life by turning pain into art" as well as a means to self-understanding. Savery also describes the importance to the invisible man of acknowledging his connection to his folk past in order for him to make a secularly existential leap to self-discovery and commitment to action.

Eleanor Lyons chooses a more limited focus, believing that Emerson is the key to the novel's concern with identity. She argues that "The American Scholar" helps students understand the invisible man's "complicity in the events that drive him underground." In Lyons's view the novel also embraces an "Emersonian affirmation of self" that leads the invisible man to assume a socially responsible role. Cushing Strout, for his part, believes that the novel is dependent on Ellison's sense of American literature, politics, history, and culture, on his understanding of the gap between America's ideal of democracy and the reality of its "legacy of slavery" and its racial problems, and on his devotion to "his craft as a novelist" and his identity "as Western man, as political being." Strout's essay attempts to ground for students and teachers these ideas both in the novel and in Ellison's essays and interviews. Christopher Sten extends the argument by positing the view that the narrator's search for identity has its roots in the American preoccupation with identity, in Ellison's admiration for jazz improvisation, and in the novel's Eriksonian notion of identity. Sten, like Strout, is also interested in the ways in which the novel's narrator is akin to and different from his creator.

The next two essays explore primarily Ellison's debt to the larger European literary tradition. Leonard Deutsch focuses on many of the works to which Ellison alludes directly, texts ranging from *The Odyssey* to *Man's Fate*, from *The Aeneid* to *A Portrait of the Artist as a Young Man*. Deutsch also points out the importance of references to the Old and New Testaments. James R. Andreas continues this approach to *Invisible Man* by grounding the novel in the Western comedic tradition. Andreas surveys the modes and methods of comedy from such diverse sources as Chaucer and Charlie Chaplin to make the point that "*Invisible Man* is infinitely rich in a comic achievement that can only be measured against the grand traditions of world literature that inspired and nourished it."

Neil Nakadate, who teaches *Invisible Man* in courses in American literature and culture, the American novel, and multiethnic literature, concludes the section by suggesting that the course in which the novel is taught inevitably shapes the course's premises and its pedagogy. Even so, as Nakadate demonstrates, when read in conjunction with other American texts, *Invisible Man* dramatizes how race, gender, class, and ethnicity determine the nature of American experiences.

The final section, "Teaching the Novel Thematically," includes three essays. John Cooke offers a cautionary note against "overteaching" the novel. Citing the novel's instruction to the individual, "Be your own father" (154), Cooke argues that readers should conduct their own "personal exploration" of the text. He then describes how names serve to introduce such themes as the narrator's quest for self-definition, his final acceptance of ambiguity, and his embracing of personal responsibility. David Vanderwerken concentrates on the prologue and the epilogue as the keys to the novel. And, finally, Mary Rohrberger offers a reading of how Ellison's use of "surrealist paradox" functions in terms of the novel's attention to sexual identity and sex roles. She also confronts the question of Ellison's "invisible" women. Rohrberger's insistence that the novel "will not yield itself readily to analysis, because the more one sees, the more there is opened up to see, and a teacher must make choices" provides a fitting conclusion to this volume, which itself ultimately dramatizes the possibilities and limitations both of literary analysis and of the choices that all of us as teachers make.

THE STUDENT AND TEACHER AS READERS OF *INVISIBLE MAN*

The Use of Culture and Artistic Freedom:
The Right of a Minority Writer

James E. Walton

At the end of the semester, following the last substantive question on the final examination in Afro-American literature, I generally like to add one more: Which work did you most appreciate reading this term? Over the past decade or so, *Invisible Man* has garnered its share of votes in this "most favored" category—but rarely have black students selected *Invisible Man* as their favorite work. In their comments on the novel during class discussions, in fact, black students have often expressed feelings of bafflement and outrage at the novel.

Like many liberal arts colleges in the Midwest, Mount Union College, located in a small residential town, is somewhat isolated and predominantly white. Black students make up less than five percent of the student population, and there are only two black professors out of seventy on the full-time faculty. When Afro-American literature is offered, during alternate years, there generally is a fair representation of minority students in the class. Only once has the class enrollment been entirely white.

The realization that minority students in my classes invariably favor works by Richard Wright, Langston Hughes, Malcolm X, and others—while blithely dismissing Ellison's—is no longer startling to me. In one way, though, it is challenging.

The challenge, of course, is not to goad students into accepting a work because the instructor decided to include it in the course or, for that matter, because the work has achieved literary acclaim. Many students, particularly minority students, once they have mastered Ellison's rich and complex metaphors, will shrink back from what they perceive to be some of the novel's implications. Looking for the coherent statement and nurturing nascent feelings of racial pride and solidarity, many students sense an element of betrayal in *Invisible Man* for its unflattering portrayal of the nameless hero's various encounters with Trueblood, Bledsoe, the Brotherhood, and Ras the Destroyer. Worse yet, in the students' view, the novel ends on a note of uncertainty and ambiguity, leaving unresolved many of the critical social and political issues it has so dramatically raised. The challenge for the instructor, then, is to get students to deal openly and honestly with Ralph Ellison.

I start my Afro-American literature course with selections from Abraham Chapman's anthology *Black Voices* and follow a rough chronological order. Having taught history for several years earlier in my career, I find it very helpful to give a brief historical outline before assigning each work. John Hope Franklin's *From Slavery to Freedom* and Franklin and Isidore Starr's *Negro in Twentieth Century America* are invaluable here. I also use August Meier and Elliott M. Rudwick's *From Plantation to Ghetto*, C. W. E. Bigsby's *Black American Writer*, Herbert Hill's *Anger and Beyond*, and, to be sure, Robert Bone's *Negro Novel in America*. *Modern Black Novelists* by M. G. Cooke is an excellent reference work. Ironically, though, the chronological order may be partly responsible for setting up certain expectations on the students' part. By the time we reach *Invisible Man*, my students are already aware of many of the West African influences on the language, the folklore, and the customs of black and white Americans; they have experienced *Native Son*; they have already come to sympathize with the youthful Richard Wright of *Black Boy*; and they have become familiar with the poems, the short stories, and the dominant themes of the Harlem Renaissance period. Ellison's novel is followed by the *Autobiography of Malcolm X* and the more recent works by contemporary black artists, many of whom espouse views often associated with what is being referred to in some circles as the new Black Aesthetic.

The reverberating sound that penetrates the very core of many minority students and, in doing so, becomes an implicit standard by which all others are measured, I am certain, is closely akin to the tone undergirding Max's powerful, if interminable, courtroom speech in defense of Bigger Thomas and, by extension, in defense of an entire race. The eloquence and the fury of Frederick Douglass, the charisma and power of Malcolm become preeminent in the minds of my students. It is little wonder that up against such a perceived standard some of the implications in Ellison's novel appear discordant at best.

To encourage my students to deal honestly with Ellison, I openly agree with them in class discussions that black Americans, as victims, have suffered from an undeniable history of slavery, disenfranchisement, and racism. I agree with them that these issues must be responsibly addressed by black artists. I share with them personal experiences from my childhood, experiences of confronting Jim Crow in the deep South, and I encourage them to share some of their pertinent experiences. The color of the instructor need not be a preemptive factor here. Only the perspective will be different, as it will be, certainly, for the many different students in the class. Students, at this juncture, need to be reassured that the instructor considers valid the approach taken by Richard Wright and other so-called protest writers whose works deal directly with social wrong. I remind them that writers historically have used their work to effect social change. The challenge for me is to get my students to accept the validity of another approach, to see that artists— albeit black artists working intimately with their culture—can legitimately use their talent, their backgrounds to accomplish other purposes. Many black students, for very understandable reasons, want to view a literary piece by a major black artist as a means of consciousness-raising. Using gentle Socratic tactics and occasionally assuming the role of devil's advocate, I work to make them see that Ralph Ellison, like all other artists, needs the freedom simply to develop his art—without making the obligatory "dues-paying" statement.

Those students who have studied American literature with me in a previous class are reminded of Emily Dickinson, her imaginative themes, and how in her poetry she was free to experiment with rhyme, grammar, and syntax; of William Faulkner, his resourceful techniques, and how he used his imagination in portraying the values, manners, and traditions of the old and the changing South; of Samuel Clemens, his keen eye, and the way he employed his prodigious imagination in telling a tale or creating a major work. The example of Bernard Malamud is of special relevance. Students are receptive to the way Malamud, for his raw material, felt free to turn to his own ethnic past, his own personal experiences, but, as an artist, was allowed to create to the very limits of his talent and his imagination. I challenge my students to see that writers like Jean Toomer, Countee Cullen, Chester Himes, Alice Walker, and, yes, Ralph Ellison, as far as the issue of artistic freedom is concerned, certainly deserve no less.

I stress to my students that the nameless hero of *Invisible Man* is involved in a search for self, a search for individuality. If this is to be a true search, I ask my students, what restrictions can we impose on the artist? What allegiance can we demand? Allegiance to his craft? Allegiance to truth? Allegiance to ideology? Does not a search for self allow for elements of discovery, acceptance, rejection?

To further underscore the nature of this search, I will sometimes lead my students to look at their own college sojourn, their own search. For some students this personal search has involved changing majors, changing academic advisers, even transferring from one school to another. College is a time when many students, not unlike the nameless hero of *Invisible Man*, question traditional wisdom. Some suffer through states of bewilderment and confusion. It is not difficult to make college students realize the importance of freedom to their search; they must be free to accept, free to reject, if they are ultimately to discover themselves. Like Ellison's hero, college students exercise this freedom when they seek brotherhood or sisterhood in social organizations on campus. Should they become disenchanted with that membership, they are free to renounce it. Minority students on my campus, even with the formation of their own special clubs and social groups, are increasing their membership in traditionally "white" fraternities and sororities, all presumably in an effort to discover their true niche. I make the point that to deny Ralph Ellison this same unlimited freedom is to hold Ralph Ellison, as an artist, in a form of artistic and literary bondage.

What I am arguing against, of course, is a tendency toward a monolithic approach to viewing literature by American black writers. Starting with a major work like *Invisible Man*, instructors can make a strong case for cultural and literary diversity, a strong case for artistic freedom. Instructors certainly should present the criticisms of the novel by Addison Gayle and others. The black aesthetic needs to be considered. The instructor, moreover, must be aware that there are two well-armed camps on both sides of this issue. Ellison, by his example, can be instrumental in pointing the way for other minority artists, in many different fields, to follow. We often speak of the influence of Eliot and Joyce on Ellison, but there is need to speak of the seminal influence a major artist like Ellison can have on other minority writers, artists who, like the nameless hero, may venture beyond the "unseen lines" in the development of their craft. For balance, I also provide my students with excerpts of some of the author's own views on the issue of artistic freedom from *Shadow and Act* and various Ellison essays and interviews.

I require a special project of my students, one that usually involves an oral presentation. A panel made up of several students may elect, for example, to critique a short play or an appropriate critical piece. "The World and the Jug," included in *Shadow and Act*, is excellent for this purpose. Ralph Ellison clearly is his own best spokesperson on the use of culture and artistic freedom. In this essay Ellison repudiates the example of Richard

Wright, asserting that Wright subscribed to the "much abused idea that novels are 'weapons' " (114). With brutal frankness Ellison drives the point home: "No, Wright was no spiritual father of mine" (117). Ellison, instead, embraces Eliot, Pound, Faulkner, Hemingway; he claims them as his literary "ancestors" (140). "I can only ask," Ellison intones, "that my fiction be judged as art; if it fails, it fails aesthetically, not because I did or did not fight some ideological battle" (136–37).

Using a panel made up of several students is an approach that works. In allowing students to confront the issues more directly, it removes the instructor from center stage and enables the students not only to hear their peers speak forthrightly on these concerns but to hear themselves speak as well. Some of them are embarrassingly surprised to hear their own voices, to hear their own logic. The result, invariably, is that some positions are reinforced while others are just as readily reshaped.

I also read aloud to my students relevant parts of the interview between Allen Geller and Ralph Ellison, recorded in Bigsby's *Black American Writer*, in which Ellison decries the role of novelist as necessary spokesperson for a political cause. Again, I encourage students to reflect, to make comparisons, to support their stands.

There may never be a consensus among students, but many of the vocal ones seem to be more accepting of the notion that minority writers must be able to exercise complete freedom in the practice of their craft. The sophisticated black and white students of this decade, differing from their counterparts of the 1960s, appear to be less insistent, less dogmatic in their discussions on this central issue. Having already encountered *The Color Purple* and *Song of Solomon*, two popular and highly imaginative novels by minority writers, these students come to their first class already somewhat favorably disposed to the notion of artistic freedom for all. As an instructor I now feel more comfortable—much more comfortable than I did in the late 1960s—trying to get students to attain what I consider to be a more balanced view of Ellison and other minority writers who, in their work, project this sense of freedom, this sense of experimentation.

Perhaps, as one student remarked, it is still "a little too soon" for American black artists to eschew completely the political and the social in their work. (I feel compelled to add that in no way is such a position being suggested here.) There is, however, the growing acknowledgment among contemporary students that American black artists, in addition to using their racial background to make a social or political statement, can legitimately use their racial past as a productive canvas for their free artistic expression.

Making *Invisible Man* Matter

Walter Slatoff

I teach *Invisible Man* toward the end of a course on the modern American novel in which I lecture to anywhere from eighty to one hundred and fifty Cornell University students. Perhaps a third are English majors, and between none and three are likely to be black. Normally I devote three fifty-minute lectures to the book; they are followed by a fourth meeting given to students' questions and comments and an effort on my part to touch on some more problematic aspects of the book that I skim past in the lectures, especially the extent to which the young man is symbolic and realistic, representative and individual. Given the space limits here, I cannot reproduce the lectures and only attempt to describe them. My chief aim in class is to heighten my students' sense of engagement with the book and the problems it exposes—in a word, to make the book matter. *Invisible Man* is a far more angry and tormented work than it is sometimes taught to be, and I want my students to be much troubled by it.

I begin my first lecture by explaining that I have always found *Invisible Man* a particularly difficult book to talk about because I've never been able to get much distance from it. It is as if I were reading a book about a war while still in the middle of that war. And I go on to explain my conviction that most of the problems the book dramatizes are still very much with us, far more desperately so than is commonly recognized. I suggest that my lack of distance is probably a good thing, that perhaps the worst fate for the book would be for it to be responded to primarily as "a great piece of literature" and not an immediate communication that gets you all mixed up and incapable of any easy ordering of your ideas. I note how much the book itself warns against imposing our usual ideas and patterns on reality.

When I say it must be read as an immediate communication, I am thinking not only of the continuing racial problems in this country and the need for listening at all levels to the voices of black people but also of a crucial quality of the book itself: that the narrator isn't just telling a story but is talking to us about it, often in a very direct way. Here I develop and illustrate at some length the I-you pattern so prominent in the prologue and epilogue. I read the last two paragraphs of the former:

> I can hear you say, "What a horrible, irresponsible bastard!" And you're right. I leap to agree with you. I am one of the most irresponsible beings that ever lived. Irresponsibility is part of my invisibility; any way you face it, it is a denial. But to whom can I be responsible, and why should I be, when you refuse to see me? . . . Responsibility rests upon recognition, and recognition is a form of agreement. . . . But what did *I* do to be so blue? Bear with me. (14)

Then I read two passages from the epilogue: "You won't believe in my invisibility and you'll fail to see how any principle that applies to you could apply to me. You'll fail to see it even though death waits for both of us if you don't" (567); and the novel's last line, "Who knows but that, on the lower frequencies, I speak for you?" Finally, I remind my students that Whitman's "Song of Myself" begins with the word *I* and ends with the word *you* and spend a few moments comparing and contrasting the opening and closing lines of the two works.

Even more important than the direct speaking tone and I-you dialectic, I suggest, is that the telling is, itself, a way of surviving for the hero of the book, a way of handling his anger and bitterness, of staying somewhat human, of forcing himself to love as well as to hate. I illustrate here by reading aloud the entire paragraph that begins, "So why do I write torturing myself . . ." (566), and talking about it at some length. In addition to the cathartic and possibly redemptive aspects of the telling, I note the confusion and pain it entails and the ironies involved in the effort since the narrator knows that one of the tricks of those who controlled him was to keep him hoping. I suggest further that the word *torturing* is no mere literary exaggeration and that what most governs the tone of the book is a kind of torment—the kind that comes from looking at yourself as unsparingly and honestly as you can, from recognizing that you haven't solved the crucial problems you are examining, from knowing that you are still terribly enmeshed with what you have undergone, and from refusing to accept phony answers or resolutions. What we are witnessing ultimately in this book (and in certain other black writers like James Baldwin) is the effort of a person to cope fully with the mental and emotional damage caused by having grown up black in a white society—the effort of such a person, that is, to stay sane.

This is no mere liberal platitude, I insist, and ask, How does one go through what the young man has experienced in this book without going crazy? You can, in the terms of the book, remain frozen, keep your eye on the white line, keep running; but once you seriously let yourself be human, real chaos threatens. Here I read the passage in which the young man summarizes his experience in terms of freezing and thawing and speaks of the ice as melting into a flood in which he threatens to drown (253–54). Sometimes I talk a bit about similar images in James Baldwin's essays and suggest that both Ellison and Baldwin have allowed themselves to thaw and let the flood come and then faced the nearly impossible task of staying mentally (and sometimes rhetorically) afloat. What I am saying is that the damage done to many black people goes far beyond the infliction of poverty and the other usual injuries sometimes recognized by the white world. What they face, and what this book is mostly about, I repeat, is the struggle to become human and stay sane. Here I explore in some detail the insanity and real chaos of the veterans of the Golden Day saloon, the implications of the "Supercargo" and superego that "censor" and control them, and the final hysteria (laughter and tears) of the "crazy" brain surgeon. I expand a bit on the nature of hysteria and note parenthetically how, when the young man isn't frozen, nearly every aspect of his experience seems to call for both laughter and tears and how laughter is often what does enable him to cope.

How do you stay sane, I ask, after going through even the single experience of the smoker described in the opening chapter: an experience involving fighting your own kind, blindness, sex, drunkeness, scrabbling for money, electric shocks, humiliation and reward, simultaneous hatred of whites and other blacks and of yourself, the acceptance of a briefcase containing a scholarship given to you by men you have to hate and fear and who you know have contempt for you for taking it, and unbearably conflicting feelings toward a nude white dancer—wanting

> at one and the same time to run from the room, to sink through the floor, or go to her and cover her from [your] eyes and the eyes of the others with [your] body; to feel the soft thighs, to caress and destroy her, to love her and murder her, to hide from her, and yet to stroke where below the small American flag tattooed upon her belly her thighs formed a capital V. (19)

How do you stay sane, I ask, when in addition to the problems of identity everyone faces growing up, you must face the further problems that you have no name or that your name is that of your former slave masters; that you have been taught to despise the traditions and ways of being that have been part of the little identity you do have; that even when you have learned not to despise those traditions, you can't find an identity that seems helpful or relevant in the world as you see it about you. It is true, I explain, that the young man does learn not to be ashamed of Mary Rambo and that he comes to see her as "a force, a stable, familiar force" like something from his past that prevented him "from whirling off into some unknown which [he] dared not face" (252). And he gains a wonderful sense of freedom when he unashamedly eats yams on the street, a sense of freedom associated with the ability to laugh and perhaps with the power he is able to exert at the eviction of the old black couple. But his new awareness doesn't help enough, as we learn from the passage in which he sadly thinks how, now that he no longer feels ashamed of the things he has always loved, he probably can "no longer digest very many of them." Realizing that he can't live simply at the yam level, he finds the end of the yam unpleasant, "frost-bitten" (260–61).

The same thing is true, I point out, when he accepts the gift of Brother Tarp's leg chain and understands it as a "paternal gesture which at once joined him with his ancestors, marked a high point of his present, and promised a concreteness to his nebulous and chaotic future" (380). But he doesn't know what to do with the leg chain except to use it as an equivalent of brass knuckles, a keepsake that offers a kind of strength and self-protection, but no direction. And the young man in this book, at least, can find no identity with his African past. He can listen to Ras the Exhorter with a degree of sympathy and understanding but sees him finally as absurd and irrelevant, dangerous and sad (552).

How do you find identity, I ask, and keep sane, when you are essentially invisible as an individual self, when no one ever asks you what you want, not even the Brotherhood through which you had hoped to gain identity? And, finally, how, if you do somehow stay sane and don't freeze up again or become numb, can you avoid either some sort of Rinehart-like cynicism where you just feed on the hopes of others or the conclusion that everything is simply absurd and the only way to manage is to opt out and move underground?

The book does not, I say, give an answer or much hope; well, maybe a small ray of hope that I'll come to later. And I go on to suggest that certain kinds of human damage can't be repaired, that all the king's horses and all the king's men can't put Humpty-Dumpty together again. (I comment a bit on the truth and relevance of nursery and folk rhymes throughout the book.)

At this point I devote considerable time to explaining that the damage is as irreparable as it is because the young man was never encouraged or even allowed to discover what he wanted and that this meant he had no self to fall back on even when he saw through what was being done to him. (Before going on to illustrate, I talk briefly about the extent to which the young man is a representative or symbolic character as opposed to an individual one in this respect and point to ways he is unlike many of his peers, especially in relation to women.) Early on he recognizes in a dream that the whites' objective is to "Keep This Nigger-Boy Running" (33), but he doesn't know what else to do. His grandfather's cryptic message—Uncle Tom them to destruction—gives no positive guidance. The same thing is true when he is unjustly punished by Bledsoe for taking Mr. Norton to Trueblood's cabin and the Golden Day, for despite his anguish and anger, he "knew of no other way of living" (144); the alternative is chaos. And the same is true with respect to his awareness that the Brotherhood is exploiting him, something he recognizes almost from the start. He holds on to the organization partly because of personal ambition and an ideal of success, values that others had taught him, but even more because a break with it would confront him with an impossible choice: one between the chaos of a mind deprived of any sense of identity and filled only with conflicting and contradictory ideas—an "old self" that was not a real self but a kind of nightmare "that flew without wings and plunged from great heights" (371)—and an alternative chaos of "falling outside of history" as Clifton does, "to plunge . . . To plunge!" (424).

The damage is irreparable also, I continue, because he can't find a way either to ignore his grandfather and all the other Sambo figures or to accept them fully. He keeps trying to throw away the Sambo coin bank he finds in Mary Rambo's house but can't get rid of it. He wants both to laugh at the Sambo dolls Clifton is selling and to destroy them (here I read the description of the dolls, trying to mimic Clifton's spiel [421–22], and emphasize that it is not an abject doll, that its very act of self-degradation is a defiance, that like his grandfather, the doll could be said to "Yassuh them to death"). The invisible man's ultimate dilemma is that the doll is a part of his heritage but one he can neither deny nor accept. To deny it is one kind of nonhumanity; to accept it is another kind of dehumanization. And the choices are fraught with danger. The white crowd loves Sambo, but when the white cop calls Clifton "nigger" and he turns on the cop like a man and not a Sambo, the cop shoots him.

And here, I insist, is the essence of that irreparable injury. The white world of the past gave the black man no alternatives between being Sambo and being dead, and at the same time it despised him for being Sambo. Then it said to Sambo's children and grandchildren and great grandchildren: If you can learn to be like us and despise Sambo, too, we'll let you share in some of our goodies. And then the white world wonders why so many black people won't buy it. I've yet to hear, I say to my usually ninety-seven-to-one-hundred-percent-white class, a word of good advice from a white man on how a black man is to come to terms with his grandfather. I certainly don't know the answer. With respect to black women, I scarcely know the relevant question.

I admit, however, that the book is perhaps not as bleak as I've been indicating, and I talk about two rays of hope. One is the young man's capacity for laughter and humor, which I emphasize by reading a number of the passages where he deals humorously with difficult problems: his discovery of the content of Bledsoe's letter (191), his reveries about Bledsoe as a chitterling eater (258–59), and his reflections about the drunken brother's request that he sing (205–06). I also talk about the humorous aspects of the prologue and epilogue, humor laced with bitterness and a sense of absurdity, but still humor.

The other ray of hope, I suggest, is that despite his having decided that the whole struggle is essentially absurd and that he is invisible, the narrator continues to recognize that invisibility is a kind of sickness and that to remain human he has to love as well as hate. And he wants to feel human. At the end of the book, although it means more pain and conflict than remaining underground, he is planning to come out of his hole, to try again. Even though he is quite sure it is no use, that "[y]ou won't believe in my invisibility and you'll fail to see it even though death waits for both of us if you don't" (567), he will try to become visible. I then propose to my students the question whether they think he should come out to try again, and I ask, "Would you?"

Finally I try to say something about the closing passage: "And it is this which frightens me: Who knows but that, on the lower frequencies, I speak for you?" It is a difficult passage, I suggest, because it means many different things and resonates in so many different directions. On one level, it seems clear enough: as we grow up (and later too), we all face the problem of discovering our selves, our identities, who and what we are and what we want as opposed to what others (parents, schools, peers) tell us we are or should be like or should want. It is also clear that we are all invisible to some degree in the sense that others tend to see us under classificatory headings rather than as individuals—as students, professors, townies, gown-ies, artsies, aggies, jocks, WASPs, Jews, New Yorkers, hicks, and so on. Even those who know and care about us tend to see us in their own terms, categories, and images rather than in our own. And yet none of these more obvious sorts of explanations seem fully to warrant the scariness of that final "it is this which frightens me."

I explain then that while I can't make a fully logical connection between that ending and what I am about to say, a certain thought keeps coming into my head each time I read the passage and think about invisibility. What I think about is the incredible extent to which people do not look at one another, do not do so in most communities and especially on my own campus; the extent to which we—professors and students alike—act as though we do not see one another and are not seen, act in such a way as to make ourselves and others invisible. And that seems scary to me, something to be afraid of. Is that perhaps what the invisible man is finally most afraid of—that terrible tendency in *all* of us to inflict invisibility on others and in some sense to choose it? Why do we do this? What is it we're so afraid of? The discomfort of being and feeling human?

Discovering an Art of the Self in History:
A Principle of Afro-American Life

John M. Reilly

Whether or not they are conscious of possessing a theory of literature, most undergraduate students will intuitively approach a novel with an expectation that plot only thinly disguises the author's experiences and that when the text recounts social conditions, it can be readily translated as a confirmation of the findings of sociology or history. If the text has been written by an Afro-American, students become all the more confident of the validity of their approach, for popular awareness of racial injustice lends weight to the verisimilitude of the fiction, making it seem self-evident that the writer's literary motive is to testify against oppression. As a teacher I am, of course, encouraged by the students' assumption of an intimate connection between literature and society as well as by their conviction that fiction has political value. At the same time, though, I am compelled to challenge their assumption, a commonsense version of the reflection theory of literature, in order to argue that literature is more proposition than report. To put it another way, and to relate my purpose to *Invisible Man*, I want to forestall their reading of the novel as an empirical instrument for recording reality, a manner of reading that tends to dissolve the text into paraphrase. Without denying truth value in the text or suggesting that the novel exists autonomously in a realm of its own, I want students to notice the text, to see that Ellison's conception of self and life is their proper subject.

Saying that I think it is necessary to challenge the students' initial approach to *Invisible Man* does not mean that I conduct a debate on the relative merits of critical theory, but since sooner or later some perceptive or well-read person in a class will contribute the information that the college attended by the invisible man resembles Tuskegee Institute and the Brotherhood resembles the Communist party, I anticipate that it will be perfectly natural for study of the novel to lead to consideration not only of topical references we discover in the narrative but of Ellison's particular interpretation of their significance. Literary mediation of reality will, so to speak, form the subtext of the class discussion.

Ellison makes it easy for us to distinguish empirical from literary reality. All we need do is begin at the beginning. Examining the prologue of the novel, I try to make two fundamental points about its relationship to the rest of the book. First is the fact that the prologue occupies the "present" of the text. The main body of the narrative, though it comes second in the reader's time, occurred before the narrator went underground and can be understood as a re-creation undertaken to simulate the "past" with the aid of the reflective comprehension of hindsight. Though the idea of an author's providing a prefatory explanation of purpose will be familiar to students, in order to describe Ellison's project in detail I elaborate the significance of the fictional "present" and "past" with two analogies: the flashback in a film and the writing of an autobiography. A flashback, I explain, may be exposition of background information designed to complete the plot or to show another dimension to character. In the writing of one's life story, however, one interprets the past from a mature perspective by selecting what now appear to be crucial experiences and influences because they show how one became the teller of a tale with thematic importance. The prologue of *Invisible Man*, I say, is like the announcement of an autobiographical theme, asserting that a life once lived in uncertainty and confusion, as to some degree all lives are, has been given the plot and symbolic episodes requisite to a story.

The second point I make about the prologue, and by now I can also speak of the epilogue as part of a whole "present," is that the surreal style and imagery of its narration erase distinctions between interior and exterior reality, merging them into one, just as the pot-induced vision related by the narrator blends time and space into a single dimension. Ordinarily, brief discussion with the class establishes the plausibility of such a merger from the experience of dreams and memory. Returning to literature, I ask that we explore the implications of such a manner of narration in order to fix the premises that underlie the entire novel. Through this discussion, I propose that students view the narrative clutched between the subjective excursions of prologue and epilogue as a structure of interpretation within the mind of a narrator for whom events, and indeed his own identity, are elements that he arranges and interprets as a particular version of the collective black experience. It logically follows, then, for that person to be taken by us as Ellison's imaginative means of presenting American life.

As students become used to treating the novel as an epistemological enterprise, though that may not be how they would spontaneously label it, they have no difficulty seeing the shaping hand of the narrator within the comparatively realistic scenes of the main body of the text. With simple guidance, they uncover the richly symbolic value of such scenes as the battle royal, the Bledsoe interviews, the Liberty Paint episode, and the Brotherhood experience. The only limit on their ingenuity is the need for some principle of coherence that will suggest a pattern of development. I suggest to them that this can be found by examination of the persona in process of arriving at the condition he expresses in the prologue and epilogue.

At this point in our study of the novel we arrive at a demonstration of how some idea of mediated reality can be more useful in reading the novel than is an expectation that the narrative will directly reflect experience. The first trait of the persona students are likely to observe is his innocence. For some reason, they say, he is unable to fathom the behavior of white racists who invite him to be the object of their mockery, and he puzzles endlessly over the meaning of his grandfather's deathbed speech. Recalling the premises established by the prologue, I remind students that Ellison has created a narrator who in turn is simulating the experience of discovering the contradictions surrounding democracy in America. As readers we are as aware as Ellison is, and as is the mature persona he presents in the prologue, that the ethics of Jim Crow require separate and decidedly unequal tracks of aspiration, because the novel is structured so that Ellison may reach behind the youthful consciousness of the persona to show the cause of his troubles located in social issues.

Underlying the trait of innocence, so characteristic of autobiographical accounts of youth, as I point out, is the theme of a bildungsroman under a comic aspect. To clarify the specific operation of the traditional narrative pattern, I cite the famous passage on double-consciousness from W. E. B. Du Bois's *Souls of Black Folk*. Ellison knows the "sense of always looking at one's self through the eyes of others" (*Souls* 16–17), and through the provision of the persona in the prologue, he permits us to know it governs the career of the youthful invisible man. But for much of the central narrative, the protagonist remains convinced of the indivisible validity of the democratic principles embodied in American political philosophy. He is striving to be an American and must yet learn to see himself as others do. It is the material of comedy, bitter comedy.

In "The Art of Fiction," an interview conducted three years after publication of the novel, Ellison describes the subject of his book as "innocence and human error, a struggle through illusion into reality." In explanation he points out that "maximum insight on the hero's part isn't reached until the final section." Progress toward insight, Ellison explains and I report for the class, is marked by the use of a charged fictional device: "Each section begins with a sheet of paper; each piece of paper is exchanged for another and contains a definition of his identity, or the social role he is to play as defined for him by others. But all say essentially the same thing, 'Keep this nigger boy running' " (*Shadow* 177). To amplify Ellison's explanation, I draw on *From behind the Veil*, in which Robert B. Stepto reminds us of the importance attached to written documents such as passes or protection papers in slave narratives like Frederick Douglass's *Narrative*. The pass, which Douglass and other slaves forged, provided the slave liberty to travel. In comically ironic reversal, the persona of *Invisible Man* accumulates all sorts of written documents (diplomas, letters of recommendation, etc.) that he believes identify him and grant him the liberty due a free-born American. The double-edged joke, as Stepto puts it, "is that none of these 'protections' are worth more than the paper they are written on" (173).

For comedy of the sort operating in *Invisible Man* to be effective, there must be a double vision different from that described by Du Bois. This comic vision requires awareness of a gap between the common awareness of persona and reader and the consciousness at the center of the re-created narrative. Having established the awareness of the narrative voice in the prologue and having indicated the capacity of that voice to shape and direct the story it tells in the central portion of the novel, I can now help students parallel the movement through the institutional life of America with a growth of consciousness marked by a gradual recognition that the persona contains in his mind the unreconciled strivings described by Du Bois, and also ultimately the means of reconciling them.

Since I have emphasized the relevance of the premises of the prologue and epilogue for understanding the novel, tracing the developing persona becomes a process of pursuing intratextual cross-references, especially when the class discusses the Harlem scenes and the encounter with the protean images of Rinehart in the later parts of the novel. To focus attention on the persona's rising consciousness of the possibilities of discovering or creating one's freedom, I urge students to attend to features of black culture embedded in the novel, for it will be by "willed affirmation of self . . . against all outside pressures" and by "identification with the group as extended through the individual self" (Ellison, *Shadow* 132) that the persona finds his freedom. Among the black cultural items that are easily educed are the folkloric trickster embodied in Rinehart and the many instances of oration, but above all there is the pervasive element of blues, stated in the prologue as the theme "*What did I do / To be so black / And blue?*" (12). While independent allusions to black popular culture readily emerge from reading the novel, cogent presentation of overall patterns requires the help of specialized scholarship. For me that comes to hand in the chapter on the novel in Robert G. O'Meally's *Craft of Ralph Ellison* (78–104) and in two works by Albert Murray: *The Omni-Americans* and *The Hero and the Blues*.

If my experience teaching *Invisible Man* is characteristic, most teachers find that even carefully directed class discussion threatens to go beyond the time allotted for the novel. The need to cover other important works in a course on the American novel or modern literature discourages introduction of other writings by Ellison, but if time can be found, I strongly recommend assigning some of his essays, or at least summarizing them for the class, because the approach I am outlining here includes not only interpretation of *Invisible Man* but also an attempt at a conclusive treatment of Ellison as an imaginative interpreter of America. In short, my approach requires me to finish the presentation of Ellison by elevating to primary consideration the debate between the commonsense reflectionist approach to fiction and the idea of a mediated presentation of reality.

I try to accomplish this by relating the persona of the novel to the one created in selected essays, most of them appearing in *Shadow and Act*. In the introduction to that volume Ellison declares that the basic significance of the pieces he has collected, "whatever their value as information or speculation, is autobiographical" (xviii). Taking Ellison at his word and reminding students that the prologue and epilogue of the novel can be seen as enunciations of the way an autobiographer approaches the writing of a life, I urge them to consider the importance Ellison attaches to his youth in Oklahoma, whose settlement occurred hardly more than a generation before his birth. The community he grew up in was for the time exempt from the equilibrium of rigid caste relationships, and it selected as idols jazz musicians rather than "judges and ministers, legislators and governors" (xiv). In each of these recollections, Ellison characterizes himself as an archetypal product of American frontiers, geographical and social. So, inviting students to reflect on the words in which Ellison presents himself and his childhood friends as "exploring an idea of human versatility" (xiv) and aspiring to become Renaissance figures, I suggest that the persona of *Shadow and Act* authenticates the essays in the same way that the mature narrator we see in the epilogue of *Invisible Man* authenticates the novel. They are fraternal twins.

Yet, I hasten to add, for fear that I might have suggested the novel is autobiographical, the parallels between novel and nonfiction are on the level of concepts that arise from experience but are not the experiences themselves. The essays in *Shadow and Act* embodying concepts that might be considered the source for *Invisible Man* include "Twentieth-Century Fiction and the Black Mask of Humanity," which recalls the epistemological themes of the novel in its discussion of the place of racial stereotypes in the "struggle over the nature of reality" (26); "Hidden Name and Complex Fate," which presents black culture as the exemplification of living in a zone of undiscovered possibility; and the reviews of Gunnar Myrdal's *American Dilemma* and LeRoi Jones's (Amiri Baraka's) *Blues People*, in which, by denying a view of blacks as victims to be defined entirely in relation to white society, Ellison suggests a way out of the dilemma of double consciousness posed by Du Bois.

Of course, *Shadow and Act* is at best an inceptive autobiography. There are almost no particularized data of the sort one finds in conventional life writing to describe forebears and growth, and we glimpse the plot of a life through fragments; yet, there is a presiding consciousness deeply occupied with the classical issues of American social philosophy. As I tell my classes, that consciousness assumes the dimensions of a persona as it explores the significance of writing and culture to the promise of democracy. In "Hidden Name and Complex Fate" the author-persona tells us that our nation began "not through the accidents of race or religion or geography . . . but when a group of men . . . put down, upon what we now recognize as being quite sacred papers, their conception of the nation which they intended to establish on these shores" (*Shadow* 163–64). And in a later essay, "The Little Man at Chehaw Station," in *Going to the Territory*, he establishes the site of the struggle to define American identity as "a terrain of ideas . . . that draw their power from the Declaration of Independence, the Constitution, and the Bill of Rights" (17). These references to documents clearly recall the use of documents in the main body of the novel and offer the opportunity to contrast the invisible man and the persona of *Shadow and Act* in a way that shows a profound connection between the two works. The bitter comedy marking the career of the young and innocent protagonist of *Invisible Man* derives from what might be called unsophisticated reading. He assumes that the documents, some of which he never reads, simply describe present reality. The mature protagonist of the novel comes near to the persona of *Shadow and Act* in understanding that language, including language relating the adventures of an invisible man, is a complex form of symbolic action providing, in the case of statements about democracy, positive terms for social order that must be realized by active will.

In the hope that students' expectation that a novel will exactly replicate life experience has been modified by our consideration of the personae, I try to sum up our study of *Invisible Man* in a way that will preserve the integrity of both its art and the social experience to which it is linked. No doubt there are a number of ways to do this, but here at least is an example. Citing Ellison's remarks on the art of the blues, such as the passage in "Remembering Jimmy" where Ellison states that blues are "an assertion of the irrepressibly human over all circumstances whether created by others or by one's own human failings" (246), and recalling that both the novel and the collected essays represent personae acknowledging bitter experience but transcending it by affirming the power to control one's own destiny, I declare that through the aesthetic practice of Ralph Ellison we have located a principle of Afro-American life that no factual documentation will allow us to share so well—the capacity of deliberate art to found a zone of freedom.

Learning to Listen to Lower Frequencies

Gordon O. Taylor

Hark ye yet again,—the little lower layer.
Moby-Dick, 1851

Who knows but that, on the lower frequencies, I
speak for you?
Invisible Man, 1952

For a long time I *didn't* teach Ralph Ellison's *Invisible Man*. This was due in part to my not having encountered the novel in an English course as an undergraduate at Harvard (1956–60) or as a graduate student at Berkeley (1960–66). One tends initially, I think, to teach what one has been taught, however differently. It was also due in part to a certain lack of awareness or curiosity in myself during those years, the book having appeared in 1952 whereas I finally read it almost fifteen years later.

In a number of ways, personal and professional, I regret this inattention at the time to what even then was recognized by many as a significant American literary event. In other ways, however, I'm glad I first read *Invisible Man* at some distance from the categories into which one felt, during student years, to some degree obliged to fit each new text, whether reading it for a class or running across it on one's own. I'm also glad that I read it some time before it occurred to me to teach it, or before I understood that it was essential that it be taught, and in a broad variety of ways. Even as my Harvard instructors, presenting me as a freshman with *The Education of Henry Adams*, intoned that book's importance to "any serious student of American civilization" (not that many freshmen are ready for the role), so I, presenting *Invisible Man* to my students at whatever level, am likely now to claim for Ellison's book a similar value as a milestone in the making of American consciousness. (Worlds apart in time, circumstance, and reasons for writing as Adams and Ellison may have been, *Invisible Man* and the *Education*—each with an author-protagonist in quest of reliable truth on which to ground a sense of self and a vision of the world, each stripping back layerings of reality and illusion in the process, "history" for each an ungraspable phantom as well as a structure of everyday life—may perhaps be profitably compared. This is not really the occasion for such a comparison, although the thought bears some relation to what I shall say later about teaching *Invisible Man* together with autobiographical, rather than only with fictional, texts.) But on first coming to Ellison's novel—even if later than most of my professional generation—I was without specifically professional purpose, merely a reader reading. An innocent, shall we say?

Which brings me to other, perhaps truer reasons for my not having attempted to teach *Invisible Man* for so long, which in turn underlie my present sense of how the novel might be taught, or taught anew in each new situation. In my innocence more than my belated professional experience, I was stunned by the power of both novel and novelist, by the contrapuntal craft of the book and the white heat of its author's urgent voice. I saw the narrative as aesthetically contained, coiled tensely yet deliberately between prologue and epilogue, ready in having found its angle of repose. By contrast, I felt the narrator's presence as filled with unresolved tension, furious both with determination and despair, the pressure of his speaking voice threatening at every moment the composition of the written words, the human issues somehow inimical to those of art.

Much as I may now look back and see this gap between aesthetic composure on the one hand, and the volatility of personal incompletion on the other, as precisely the field of force from which the act of Ellison's art proceeds, I was daunted then as well as compelled by the difference. Much as for me now the relation between novelist and narrator is one of subtle mixtures of identity and distance, then it was one of cruder, if no less crucial, polemic alliance, the author embattled through the means of his persona and, because of the intensity of his personal concerns, with his own artistic ends. My sense of my own relation as reader to both narrator and novelist —of listening to the voice speaking to and perhaps "for" me, and from it learning something of how to speak about the book myself—would come later.

Far from disclaiming such initial impressions, I continue to find in them sources of what I now presume to think a more refined sense of the problems and the opportunities involved in teaching *Invisible Man*. Both early impressions and current perceptions converge, perhaps, in the energizing tension between an unfinished and inherently unstable human process in which Ellison and his invisible man are distinct yet one—a process of self-definition as an American, a black, a literary artist or an artist of the self, and, subsuming all, as a human being—and the ostensible stability of a finished artifact. For the moment, however, my point is that the novel seemed to me at first to defy critical approach (and therefore also pedagogical approach, had I been thinking of this then) by transcending, even while remaining firmly anchored in both art, as an end in itself, and a seemingly insoluble dilemma of racial consciousness, spelling the end of an idea of America.

Time, familiarization with the text, and some accumulation of experience as a teacher of American literature inevitably led me to introduce *Invisible Man* into courses without necessarily resolving these conflicts in my own ideas about the book. On the surface of things, once I did begin to teach it, the question became, How was one to present this novel at Harvard or Berkeley in the late sixties or early seventies, when the immediate problem seemed to be persuading many students that the recurrent use of the word *nigger* by Huckleberry Finn did not necessarily make of Mark Twain a racist or of his book a racial affront? Beneath the surface, of course, was that aspect of Ellison's book through which one might have addressed precisely such misapprehensions of Clemens's tale. Unrecognized at the time, this opportunity in turn was rooted in *Invisible Man's* continuing challenge to its own categories: of genre and technique, fictional and personal narrative; of modernism and postmodernism, Afro-American and American literature; of literature itself in relation to oral or folk tradition; of racial in relation to human identity. The challenge was also, and still is, to the teacher's capacity, in presenting this (or *any?*) work, to allow it to teach its readers how it requires to be read, by enabling them to listen as well as to see, to hear as well as to analyze and understand.

In other words—and in sounds and silences other than words—Louis Armstrong's jazz, into the breaks in which (as it is put in the prologue) the reader must slip along with novelist and narrator in order to "grasp invisibility," is part and parcel of the text; not just the reference to "What Did I Do to Be so Black and Blue," but the song itself, and in turn the largely unwritten musical literature from which it largely derives. So also, therefore, "There's Many a Thousand Gone" is integral to Ellison's text, not just as a song heard at Tod Clifton's funeral but as a moment in the unwritten, unbroken song of sorrow from which the particular spiritual springs, receding into the past yet informing Armstrong and Ellison alike. We don't read it —the words aren't there—we hear it without knowing the words in something like the sense in which we hear more than we read the voice of Huckleberry Finn, but more in the way in which we take in the epigraphic bars of music, standing for slave songs, as we enter each chapter of Du Bois's *Souls of Black Folk*. The spirituals weren't written, even as musical notation, at the time from which emanate the strains Du Bois wants us to hear. Their burden as an overriding, underlying composite "text" was nonetheless contemporary for him in 1903, when *Souls* was published, and still so in 1953, as is clear from his preface to a later edition appearing almost simultaneously with *Invisible Man*. So too a printed title—"What Did I Do to Be so Black and Blue" (8)—shifts in Ellison's prologue to phrasing at once heard and intoned by the narrator—"*What did I do / To be so black / And blue?*" (12). The rhetorical question is then dispersed into "the invisible music of my isolation" (13), an entire novel its attempted answer, with the reader of necessity immersed in the attempt.

"At first I was afraid," says the invisible man, of the action seemingly demanded by this "familiar music" (12). Familiar as I may have become with the book after a time, I still feared it, and mistrusted myself with it, even as I was powerfully drawn to and moved by it. No doubt I was nervous early on, as a white teacher of mostly white students at an uneasy moment in American social history, a sense of which the novel seemed prophetically to contain, however clearly it also referred to an already established pattern of racial conflict in America. Deeper, however, was another sort of uncertainty, which still exists but which now motivates more than it obstructs my teaching of this text: how to handle the terrific tension between the literary and the social issues, between matters of aesthetic effect and matters of moral consequence? This tension, which exists in all Ellison's writing, is also the tension between, on the one hand, the self-creative act of writing, speaking, even just thinking oneself into being in a world as it ought to be, into an imagined, hoped-for America, and, on the other hand, the precarious, survivalist art of reading the world as it really is, an actual America fraught with danger for the misreader as well as open to the possibility of new interpretation. "Build therefore your own world," said the poet of "Nature" (Emerson, *Selections* 56) exhorting us to the self-creative act, knowing the personal and societal risks, even the impossibility, of such an undertaking, in the face of the world's obdurate facts.

Ellison too—with an Emersonian inheritance of his own lying deeper than the link in his given names, Ralph Waldo, deeper also than his antagonism toward the character Emerson in the novel—sees the world, and the self in the world, both ways. Author, protagonist, and reader of *Invisible Man* alike, teacher and student together as well, are at once trapped and deliberately positioned in the space between reality and illusion, each of which appears in both benign and malignant aspects. Layers of self-delusion and deception by others are peeled back, toward the core of self from which the narrator will strive to build his own world anew yet will also seek to deal, be required to deal, with the world as it stands. The process is one in which both writer and reader are complicit, more than by reason of the one's portrayal or the other's apprehension. The invisible man's question—"So why do I write, torturing myself to put it down?" (566)—in its outcry and in its calmer, more inward reflection (like Louis Armstrong's "What did I do . . . ?"), both rhetorically voices our shared predicament and calls on us to listen, on lower frequencies within ourselves as well as in the resonances of text, for our individual answers. It is not necessarily promised that the task will become easier or that the painful intensity of the effort will subside. It is only granted, to those for whom the writing, the speaking, the reading and thus the teaching have become a single, ongoing, interconnected act, that it will seem important to continue.

Continuing for me has thus become a tendency, pronounced if not invariable, toward presenting *Invisible Man* less in the context of the American novel and its tradition than in that of American personal narrative, in a sense that need not exclude fiction or indeed any other genre. I teach it not *as* autobiography (although it rings "true" as personal account to a degree that might make an actual autobiography from Ellison, perhaps even another novel, seem superfluous) but, rather, as a work related to various other works of autobiographical expression, whether or not strictly speaking of autobiography as such, by black authors: Douglass, Du Bois, Johnson, Hurston, Wright, Baldwin, Malcolm X, to name a few. And not black writers alone, as my mention of Adams, Clemens, and Emerson, along with other references below to more recent white figures, may indicate. The voicing of black self and black experience is the issue closest to the center of the materials I will often cluster around Ellison in preparing a course. But it is also, inherently in the materials themselves rather than as a pedagogical thesis, a primary means through which Ellison and others claim personal and literary identity in a larger American context and, as Americans, carry out their critical analyses of America.

Across a broad spectrum of ethnic, regional, social, or intellectual issues or concerns, this drive to differentiate oneself, and at the same time to take one's place in a community that itself is still incompletely defined, has from the beginning been a primary impulse in American literary culture. For Ellison and his invisible man it is both means and end, an abiding theme that generates other themes as, conversely, tributaries feed a main river, a "mainstream" if you will. It has been an abiding theme from Douglass to Malcolm X, from the oldest slave narratives and sorrow songs through the self-liberating stories of, say, Alice Walker. Walker's recent *In Search of Our Mother's Gardens* renews yet again the link with the past while asserting her freedom from it, asserting also her presence in a literature from which her forebears were forcibly absent, both as women and as blacks. So Baldwin inserts himself into the "white centuries" of European (hence American) history. So Ishmael Reed, characteristically contrary, defies his readers to see him as ever having been removed from history, from the world as it is, if only through the sheer force of his self-projection into the world as he would have it be. (If to create oneself in personal narrative is to confront the task of surviving in the world one has imagined—surviving for the very purpose of sustaining the narrative—might there not be a connection between Reed in his multiple personae and that of his Melvillean namesake, as perhaps between Ellison and Emerson? Or, for that matter, between Ellison and Melville?—Ishmael forever doomed yet dedicated to speaking "for" us in having "ESCAPED ALONE TO TELL THEE," in the epilogue, which draws the lower layers of the narrator's experience back through the narrative and into his opening words. "Call me Ishmael." "I am an invisible man.") Surely this is also an abiding theme in American literature as a whole, colonial, classical, modern, and contemporary.

The example of *Invisible Man* is in this regard supreme. It binds itself into, rather than isolating itself from, American social and moral experience, into the patterns of American literary practice, not that these are always one and the same. And it does so by insisting on the depth and comprehensive American applicability, the universal human significance, of its racial theme. Only in this sense does Ellison "transcend" (and still less in his public presence as a writer has he disregarded or abandoned) the matter of race. His novel plumbs, more than it either presumes to resolve or despairs of resolving, the persistent ambiguity between the professed values and the actual assumptions awash in the American psyche and apparent in America's social behavior. In doing so, the novel both asserts and subverts the power of art, its redemptive force or its self-sufficiency as a motive ("So why do I write . . . ?"), subverting at least that art which would claim to have brought American actualities and potentialities into perfect alignment. Would not Rinehart, like Malcolm X in his earlier street-hustling days, be in that sense the "perfect" artist of the self, a narrator in a world of pure, absolute possibility, a transparent eyeball with shades?

The world of the invisible man has by the end "become one of infinite possibilities" (563), yet the distinction he draws between himself and Rinehart, while fine, is absolute. The true artist must like Rinehart master chaos, "to the destructive element submit" (Stein's injunction in Conrad's Lord Jim [130]), explore the emptiness of what Dickinson called "The Missing [Emersonian] All," move through that borderless zone. The true artist must also, however, remap its borders without losing sight of the chaos they contain, conceive a plan of living without denying death, condemn and affirm, hate and love, say no and say yes. Emerge. "So I approach it through division" (567), he says, and there is something in this for us as teachers of the book.

Invisible Man manifests—which is a way of probing—the instabilities of relation between the knowledge of human failure and the notion of limitless human aspiration, between honorable if inevitable shortcomings of effort toward the ideal and ignoble, unforgivable betrayals of the ideal. This even in a world—"contemporary" as distinct from "modern"?—from which such abstract Faulknerian verities seem in their abstraction, in the turning of a gyre, to have disappeared. Taking *Go Down, Moses* and *Invisible Man* as predicated respectively on modern and postmodern assumptions about the nature of reality, I have sometimes placed both books at the start of a course on contemporary American writing. It works—Ellison's narrator's predicament and quest are more similar in the end to, say, Oedipa Maas's in Pynchon's *Crying of Lot 49* than they are to the situation of those blacks whose history is submerged in Isaac McCaslin's obsessive quest to redeem it. Yet even in such a course, even with Ellison's as the only "black" book, *Invisible Man* serves not just to chart the racial tributary entering the mainstream, not just as an individual masterpiece equal to any, but also as a superconductor charged almost to overload with the energy of American imagination, past, present, and future.

When the narrator asks "But how shall I live?" (simply an economic question in context) on his release following electroshock treatment (241), the reader hears, on a lower frequency of sorts, the perplexity of Malcolm X, which also surpasses its immediate context, when he asks, "How is it possible to write one's autobiography in a world so fast-changing as this?" (408). One may also hear Maureen asking, in Joyce Carol Oates's *Them*, "How can I live my life if the world is like this?" (330). In each case, as in that of Ellison's narrator, perplexity or despair—active or inert, knowing or naive—exists within a plan of living, a pattern of shifting certainties, an answer shaped against as well as by a question. Each speaker inhabits both the world as it is and the world as it might otherwise be, one deadly if not understood, the other powerfully capable of being born in either imagination or delusion. Like the invisible man itemizing light bulbs, building and furnishing a house to last forever yet also to be sloughed like old skin, each is with the highest seriousness, and on the lowest levels of confluence with American tradition, coming to know and trying to tell—or rather learning in the act of telling —Where I Lived and What I Lived For.

Reader reading, teacher teaching are subject to the same conditions of isolation and uncertainty as those faced by writer writing and speaker speaking, through which nonetheless all must, will, purposefully move. The classroom becomes a community (a little commonwealth? a raft on a river? the Rachel in her retracing search? orphans of a failed Brotherhood?), each member of which plays an individual part in responding to the power of its common text, the urgent words that have become its demanding world. This superabundant force, undeniable as the noonday sun, bears out from the center of *Invisible Man*, against its formal boundaries and its sense of the limits of personal and social possibility. It finally resides in the words set in epigraph at the outset of this essay, words at once conjectural and absolute, with which the book concludes without coming to rest: "Who knows but that, on the lower frequencies, I speak for you?" Here at the end the narrator only seems to be speculating. He does speak for us, and he will be heard, whether or not we have yet learned to see him or receive his signal; he will be heard, too, on our collective American behalf as much as on his own in adverse relation to America.

His words themselves issue from a kind of fear ("And it is this which frightens me," he says by way of preface to them). It is his own fear of resurfacing in a world within which he is committed to a continuing role, to the action he initially fears in the prologue. Perhaps it is Ellison's fear of emergence or separation, his act of writing done, from a world of text in which the end is in the beginning and still lies far ahead. Both Ellison and his invisible man fear for America; and to stay in the hole, to not quite yet have finished or begun again the work at hand, is in some measure to allay that unrest. In this they share a double fear: on the one hand, of after all projecting only a puppet voice, set up to be dismissed as "buggy jive" by an unseeing, unhearing white America; on the other hand, of discovering that in its heart of darkness, in the blood, white America so deeply and unanswerably recognizes, or fails to recognize, the truth as projected here that only violence will clear the ground for a new beginning. Such a beginning would be foretold in the end and thus lie far behind, a future foreclosed. Finally, perhaps savingly, there is the fear of which I have spoken as a teacher, in its way a fear of speaking "for" others whose experience of the novel, or of the world, is as authentic as my own, even while speaking to them about my sense of either or both. The invisible man is a teacher teaching too.

Richard Wright, in *American Hunger*, faces with terror as well as both rage and exhilaration the blank sheet of paper on which he must continue to inscribe his being. In Baldwin's version of this image, recurrent in black American autobiography, the self-creating writer who would create the consciousness of others must at this point risk all—"Everything now . . . is in our hands"—and by achieving the self "achieve our country, and change the history of the world" (*Fire* 119). In hope as well as in anger and fear, Ellison and the invisible man—our secret sharer as much as his—risk the white space between the epilogue's last word and the prologue's first, between the world he knows and the world he dreams. He dares the reader to reenter that medium, to accept yet still seek to change the history of the world, to listen yet again and this time hope to hear. To teach *Invisible Man*, no less than to read it for a first or a fiftieth time, is to accept the challenge.

A Deeper Literacy:
Teaching *Invisible Man* from Aboriginal Ground

R. Baxter Miller

Play the game, but don't believe in it—that much you
owe yourself. Even if it lands you in a strait jacket or a
padded cell.

Invisible Man 151

"Just tell him that I said the grass is green . . ."
"What?"
"The grass is green. It's our secret code, he'll
understand."

Invisible Man 102

Lately it has become somewhat fashionable to read and teach Ellison's text
as a structural achievement in Euramerican literacy (see Pancho Savery's
discussion of recent trends in Ellison scholarship in the "Materials" section
of this volume). The power of *Invisible Man*, according to this reading,
emerges from an ideological affinity to the Declaration of Independence,
the master text of American society. In such a view Ellison is one of the
greatest and most literate American authors because he completes the em-
blematic and aesthetic tradition of Emerson, Melville, Twain, and Faulkner.
But it is possible to question the theory behind this belief and assertion. In
the process we can do more than value, or indeed even love, the Euramerican
mythos on our own terms; we can approach it as something dubious, like
the supposedly empirical history of American culture and the West. Admittedly such a reading goes far beyond the ideological conservatism of
Ellison himself, a position that may have led to the important reassessment
of his masterpiece during the eighties, as the national commitment to civil
rights "boomerangs" backward to the suppression of the early fifties.

The point here is to clarify the deeper reading *Invisible Man* calls for,
which, I believe, is not a reading of grammar, or of the linguistic connections
between the scenes, or of the structure that ties each part to the whole. A
deeper reading does not come through the belief that engagement with the
text is only linear, moving from the grandfather at the beginning, through
the impersonal eviction of a black couple from their apartment in the middle,
and back to the grandfather's saying at the end. A deeper reading emerges
through an awareness that space is vertical and temporal as well as linear
and horizontal. Deep space involves consciousness and culture. Profound
reading confirms the vitality of a literacy inseparable from rhetorical history,
inseparable, in other words, from the academic and political interests pre-

scribing a democratic language and a "literate" canon. For most of us, the pressure to teach only the accepted literacy is far greater than we confess.

An immersed reading of *Invisible Man* reveals a living language informed by extrinsic circumstances that inevitably affect it. As an imperfect product of Ellison's Enlightenment kind of thought—his idea that concepts and texts divorce themselves from social agendas—such a reading unintentionally reveals a truth of another sort. Not only the source for one mythic code, for a superficial literacy, or for the reading simply of plot or the democratic code before us, the text provides an opportunity to teach the repressed code that neither the narrative voice nor the authorial one would ever concede. Hence, true literacy becomes not just the contemplative awareness of, and cowardly escape from, the fictions that others would impose on us but the assertion of our own fiction, namely, the literate power of a humane life, an assertion that enables us to redefine the conceptual and cultural dictates of our world. True literacy becomes dynamic.

It is only rudimentary to recall a basic reading for teaching *Invisible Man*. The unnamed narrator, having distinguished himself as a young orator and blind believer in the accommodationist principles of Booker T. Washington, wins a scholarship to a black college in the South. Trusted to entertain Mr. Norton, a white philanthropist of the school, he takes him to the wrong side of the tracks across a white line in the highway. There they meet Trueblood, who has impregnated his daughter, Matty Lou, during a nightmare. Afterward the storyteller takes the anxious Norton, who has repressed his hidden lusts for his own daughter, to the Golden Day saloon, where they encounter the authoritative Supercargo (Freudian superego). Subsequently expelled by Bledsoe (one of many grandfather figures, including Grandfather himself, Norton, Trueblood, Supercargo, Wrestrum, and Tarp), the invisible man, with sealed and damaging letters of recommendation from Bledsoe, makes his way optimistically to Harlem. There, after a stirring speech at the eviction of a couple from a Harlem tenement, he is recruited by the Brotherhood, a fictional counterpart of the Communist party. Duped into indirectly being part of a race riot, he withdraws into the basement of a sewer for which he taps light from the power company. After Ras and his henchmen have given up the death search for him, he anticipates a return to the surface world.

Such an overview hardly does justice to the rich complexes of image and metaphor that disclose a meaning of self and history. From the Edenic world of the school, the invisible man has fallen initially into the wasteland of experience. Here he has seen how human kind can be nearly overwhelmed by aspects of modern American life—by the machine in the boiler division of the Liberty Paint factory as well as by the political mechanism of the Brotherhood at the end of the book. Now covering his figurative scars from a fiery initiation into political reality during the "spring" of his life, he lives on. But by the end he has learned to smell the "stench" of death. His linear movement toward the North, and toward a personal search for self-meaning, parallels that of the reader toward the close of the novel.

In the title essay of *Going to the Territory*, however, even Ellison has given the structuralists a reason to read the novel only grammatically:

> Today we hear much discussion of what is termed "black English," a concept unheard of during my school days. And yet we were all the grandchildren of slaves and most of us spoke in the idioms that were native to the regions from which our families had migrated. Still, no one, much less our teachers, suggested that standard American English was beyond us; how could they with such examples as Dr. Page [first black PhD from Brown University] before us? He could make the language of Shakespeare and the King James version of the Bible resound. . . .   (137)

Would it help to quibble about the insensitivity to Western expansionism here, including the genocide of Native Americans? Such remarks, though repressed throughout Ellison's works and comments, derive in part from his belief that the frontier and Huckleberry Finn symbolize "our" culture.

But the letters that Bledsoe gives the invisible man provoke a more profound reading of a text inextricably bound to history. "That's all right," Bledsoe says to the narrator. "The school tries to look out for its own" (147). The letters are sealed, and the storyteller is not to open them if he wants help. Later, in his room in Harlem, he says, "I took off my coat and hat and took my packet of letters and lay back upon the bed, drawing a feeling of importance from reading the important names. What was inside, and how could I open them undetected?" (159). Though he knows that Bledsoe despises him for lack of foresight, and though he eventually discovers that each prospective employer from Mr. Bates through Mr. Emerson (for Ralph Waldo Ellison a well-chosen name indeed) has turned him down, he simply cannot connect the literate form of the letter to Bledsoe's agenda to "keep this nigger-boy running." His enslavement to the shape of literacy deprives him of wisdom.

Even by itself the eviction scene serves in detail to sharpen the distinction between graphically literate space (museums, the portrait of Douglass) and temporally literate space ("Barrelhouse Blues"). Here the crowd surges as white men come past, knocking over a drawer that spills its contents at the narrator's feet. Beside a bent Masonic emblem are a set of tarnished cuff links and three brass rings. Here also are a nail-pierced dime to be worn as a good-luck charm and an ornate greeting card that reads "Grandma I love you" in a child's hand. Another card shows a white man in blackface seated at a cabin door and strumming, "Going back to my old cabin home." Here are a "string of bright glass beads with a tarnished clasp," a rabbit foot, and a celluloid baseball card "shaped like a catcher's mitt, registering a game won or lost years ago." Here are an "old breast pump with rubber bulb yellowed with age, a worn baby shoe and a dusty lock of infant hair tied with a faded and crumpled blue ribbon." The narrator, nauseated by the scene, holds three lapsed insurance policies in his hand. As an initial climax, he clasps a newspaper portrait, "yellowed" like the bulb on the breast pump and probably worn or "tarnished" like the cuff links, that bears the caption "MARCUS GARVEY DEPORTED." Turning away now, he searches the dirty snow for anything his eyes may have missed. His fingers close on something "resting in a frozen footstep," the emblem of black American progress. The fragile paper, deteriorating from age, is written on in ink once black, now yellow. He reads: "FREE PAPERS. *Be it known to all men than my negro, Primus Provo, has been freed by me this sixth day of August, 1859. Signed: John Samuels. Macon*" (265–66). The invisible man, blotting out a drop of melted snow on the yellow page, puts the paper back into the drawer. With trembling hands and rasping breath, he feels as if he has run a long way or "come upon a coiled snake in a busy street" (266). Though he had rationalized to himself that slavery was something from the distant past, he knew that it was not so. Having replaced the drawer in the chest, "he pushes drunkenly to the curb":

> But it wouldn't come up, only a bitter spurt of gall filled my mouth and splattered the old folk's possessions. I turned and stared again at the jumble, *no longer looking at what was before my eyes, but inwardly-outwardly, around a corner into the dark, far-away-and-long-ago*, not so much of my own memory as of *remembered words*, of linked verbal echoes, images, *heard even when not listening at home.* (266; my italics)

However valuable any structural and formalistic literacy may be, only a profoundly cultural understanding can reveal the brilliance here. In 1847 the "Masons" had become the First Independent African Grand Lodge, and only in 1947, the year marking the first copyright of *Invisible Man*, would Jackie Robinson be allowed finally to play for the Brooklyn Dodgers. His success marked the beginning in the desegregation of major-league baseball. While the "fragile paper" of freedom once had useful value, it has only a sentimental one now. But at least the narrator still has the prospects of self-expression.

What a critic like Robert Stepto might teach as the major strength of the novel is, for me, its most pervasive flaw. Stepto writes:

Ellison . . . makes it clear that his narrator has found a way not only to stop paying for his life within what other men call reality, but also to avoid paying for his enlightenment once he has fallen outside those imposing fictions. The former discovery releases him as DuBois and others are not released from various rhetorics of progress; the latter discovery allows him to gain as few others have gained a rhetoric of liberation. (*From behind the Veil* 192–93)

Actually it takes more self-determination and commitment on our part to imprint our own fiction and style on reality than to live the other way around. In so doing the teacher or artist achieves a positive fiction in the world rather than a cowardly one below it. While Stepto has the relation between the narrative self and the world superbly correct, the value he places on the bond requires a complete reversal. Though withdrawal by the narrator means continued slavery, literate engagement could mean new freedom. Perhaps we take our chances.

For Ellison, as for any other great artist, the deepest literacy would demand the imprint of one's own fiction on American history. But the author must attempt to repress the truth still coded in that history, and most American critics, if the current scholarship is at all telling, read the presence there of nearly every writer in the "major canon," except that of Henry David Thoreau, who perhaps does protest the rules too much. What almost everyone seems to have made taboo as much as Ellison has is that an American Revolution did indeed occur. It broke with the King's English literally as well as figuratively. But the final odyssey toward literacy is neither a test of such literary skill nor even a quality of mind so much as it is the critical will to know and to face the truth. It is a test of courage: "I got up from behind the hedge in the waning moon, wet and shaken . . ." (552).

Tod Clifton, once a youth organizer for the Brotherhood in Harlem, had already disturbed the narrator regarding such literate risks:

> "No, . . . he [Ras the Exhorter, not yet turned Ras the Destroyer] won't get on the inside. Did you hear how he was talking? Did you hear what he was saying?"
> "I heard him, sure," I said.
> "I don't know," he said. "I suppose sometimes a man *has* to plunge outside history . . ."
> "What?"
> 'Plunge outside, turn his back . . . Otherwise he might kill somebody, go nuts."
> I didn't answer. Maybe he's right, I thought, and was suddenly very glad I had found Brotherhood. (368)

Having aggravated the Brotherhood, Clifton would end up selling Sambo dolls, and Ras would be a caricature riding his horse pathetically like some burlesque knight in modern times. What none of the three (Clifton, Ras, or the narrator) would ever manage is precisely the challenge Clifton had in a fleeting moment seen as possible. None of them, in other words, could remain within history and imprint a new fiction on it, at least without turning to violence or bringing down destruction on themselves.

But Frederick Douglass, whose portrait Brother Tarp hangs on the narrator's wall at the Brotherhood, did just that. He was not necessarily a greater writer than Ellison, for a single novel hardly offers a basis for comparison, but he was a far greater man than Ellison's speaker could dream of being. Through the fight with Covey and the great orations, as much as through the pictorial space of his autobiographical texts, Douglass transformed himself from object into subject. His literate life confirmed what Gwendolyn Brooks would write more than a century later: "Say that the River turns, and turn the River" (421). But even Ellison's speaker cannot manage such living literacy at the end. After Clifton's death, he wonders about three youths in front of him:

> They were men out of time—unless they found Brotherhood. Men out of time, who would soon be gone and forgotten. . . . What if history was a gambler, instead of a force in a laboratory experiment, and the boys his ace in the hole? What if history was not a reasonable citizen, but a madman full of paranoid guile and these boys his agents, his big surprise! His own revenge? For they were outside, in the dark with Sambo, the dancing paper doll; taking it on the lambo with my fallen brother, Tod Clifton (Tod, Tod) running and dodging the forces of history instead of making a dominating stand.   (430–31)

In teaching the close of *Invisible Man*, it is helpful to recall a story that Jacques Derrida tells about the flight of an arrow. Were we to take several pictures of the shot, none could possibly reveal what motion itself is. Such a hidden charge in language makes literary narrators visible to themselves and visible to their worlds, and the latter must ultimately account for their articulate presence. This invisible dynamism (but certainly no invisible man) distinguishes the narratives of Douglass, Du Bois, Wright, and often Morrison. It is this *process* in language that gives their texts an indelible force missed at the close of *Invisible Man*.

In no way should the teaching of such weaknesses tarnish the recognition of Ellison's American masterpiece. But the significance of our inquiry directs us to ask not only about the greatness of its literary form but about the substance and consequences at hand. Having fostered a deeper literacy, we could confront the questions that much current teaching and scholarship pose. Is it better, in other words, to appreciate the text for its representation of a black American suspicion about American democracy, to face a truth that Ellison unsuccessfully tries to purge from his novel? Shall we teach the text only as an admirable Afro-American fiction on Euramerican terms? Who now are the bearers of the text? Whom do they serve? Such critical inquiries, the processes of verbal fluency, emerge very well from aboriginal ground.

THE NOVEL AND ITS AFRO-AMERICAN, AMERICAN, AND EUROPEAN TRADITIONS

Invisible Man and the
American Way of Intellectual History

Wilson J. Moses

Ever since the days of the New Critics, American literary scholars have been suspicious of intellectual history. They have rightly expressed concern regarding the use of "embarrassingly antiquated" instructional techniques and modes of literary analysis. Robert B. Stepto, in the lead essay of his *Afro-American Literature: The Reconstruction of Instruction*, criticizes that style of teaching which stresses Freudian psychology, historical context, or social scientific analysis to such an extent that the text itself is lost. Nonetheless, this essay argues the legitimacy of lecturing on intellectual history when teaching recent American novels, for example, Ralph Ellison's *Invisible Man*. Ellison clearly has a sense of literary and intellectual history, but, like most of us, Ellison is capable of feigning both knowledge and ignorance, and I suspect that, like most of us, he often bluffs when disclaiming ties to Richard Wright, Booker T. Washington, Marcus Garvey, and other well-known Afro-American wordsmiths who obviously influenced him profoundly. Of course *Invisible Man* cannot be understood in terms of a self-contained Afro-American literary tradition, but that does not mean that the reader should ideally come to it without any knowledge of the traditions of Afro-American intellectual life or of Western intellectual traditions in general.

To do so would be about as satisfying as reading Milton without a knowledge of the epic tradition or of the biblical account of creation. That intellectual history bears some relation to literary instruction cannot be seriously questioned. The prefaces and footnotes, as well as the bibliographies, of such stately volumes as *The Norton Anthology of English Literature* make it clear that literary scholarship at its best never seeks to remove the work of art from its intellectual environment. Students of Afro-American literature have always been inordinately sensitive to the accusation that what they are doing is not really literary scholarship but sociology. I have always had difficulty understanding the intellectual commitments of those who make that sort of statement. Aside from the fact that good sociology is better than bad literary criticism, it seems silly to me to use the name of any academic discipline purely as a term of opprobrium. In any case, intellectual history is not sociology; it is neither *Wissensoziologie* nor "history of ideas." Both these terms have specific meanings, outlined in the works of Karl Mannheim, Robert K. Merton, and A. O. Lovejoy. Intellectual history is a less rigid concept. It refers simply to the field of scholarship that seeks to understand the relation between the evolution of ideas and the changing material environments that produce changes in ideas. Intellectual history is not inhospitable to the proposition that ideas affect environments as well; that is why its practitioners speak of influential books.

I am not certain there is any such thing as an American intellectual history, although I am convinced that intellectual history is a valid concept and that many Americans, including black Americans, have participated in it. Over the past two centuries, a respectable number of black Americans have developed literate habits and intellectual tastes. It may be reasonable to assume that reading has had some effect on them and that their opinions have been shaped by the books they have read, as well as by their racial-ethnic experience. Ellison has a great deal to share with us, in his observations on what he has read and in his debates and discussions with critics and interviewers. It is almost superfluous to add that he has much to share with us by the example of his creative practice. Both in *Invisible Man* and in the articles and interviews collected in *Shadow and Act* and *Going to the Territory*, he asserts that the concrete intellectual experiences of Afro-Americans are important as specific manifestations of universal human experiences. He demonstrates this artistically by having the protagonist of *Invisible Man* scramble spiderlike over a web of themes, which, like a spider's web, are the product of heritage, environment, and the individual activities of the spinner. It is true that if Ellison had never read *Up from Slavery* or *A Portrait of the Artist as a Young Man*, he would have written a very different kind of work. But it does not follow that the best way to teach Ellison's novel is by lecturing about other books.

Ellison's attempts of twenty years ago to disassociate himself from the dogmas of a Black Aesthetic led him to an unnecessary repudiation of any ties he might have had to a black literary tradition. I don't want to get involved in the old *ut pictura poesis* business, but I am reminded of Pyotr Ilich Tchaikovsky's attempt to disassociate himself from the nationalistic movement in Russian music. His attacks on the nationalistic pretensions of "The Five" notwithstanding, Tchaikovsky, with his borrowings from folk music and his splendid mazurkas, remains a better illustration than anyone of what we mean by a "Russian spirit" in music. Ellison may claim that he is not a part of an Afro-American literary and intellectual tradition, but the empirical evidence does not support his contention.

Ralph Ellison was once an impatient young man. Born in Oklahoma in 1914, not only in the same state as John Hope Franklin, but less than a year in advance of him, he had some of the same biases. Nineteen fifteen was the year Booker T. Washington died, and black intellectuals born around that time—I include Thurgood Marshall and Kenneth Clark in the category—grew up with an understandable hostility to any talk of separatism. When they began their publishing careers, they had little time for the older generation, unless they could mythologize them as monumental figures who were somehow "ahead of their times." They thus failed to take advantage of a whole generation of black art and scholarship. The new intellectuals were not interested in Oscar Micheaux or Sutton Griggs. Historians read only superficially, if at all, in J. A. Rogers or Benjamin Brawley. Because of the integrationist bias of the Ellison-Franklin generation, once-respected members of the black literary pantheon, like Martin Delany and Alexander Crummell, were barely mentioned or purged entirely from the textbooks. Such occurrences have been referred to as "social amnesia," but literary amnesia would better describe the antihistorical biases that dominated American letters in the form of New Criticism at the time of Ellison's coming-of-age. Although the idea of a black intellectual tradition was never completely wiped out, the tragic fact is that neither the Ellison-Franklin generation, nor the younger generation, who in turn challenged them, were as aware of the history of black intellectual and literary traditions as they should have been. But when Ellison set out to write a bildungsroman, he happened, somehow, to produce something that was quite distinctly black.

In the tradition of Henry Adams, Ellison gave us a book about education; but for reasons known only to Ellison himself, he chose to begin his story not in Quincy, Massachusetts, but in the American South and to send his hero not to Harvard but to a black college. It may or may not be important, early in a reading of *Invisible Man*, for students to be informed that Ellison spent some time at Tuskegee Institute or that the statue of the Founder, lifting the veil from the face of a kneeling slave, is reminiscent of the Booker T. Washington statue on the Tuskegee campus. Yet, because the themes of blindness and veiled vision are so important, it might be useful to call attention to these themes as they are introduced, both here and in the battle royal of chapter 1. Seeing a picture of the Booker T. Washington statue might be of interest to students, but it is certainly important for them to understand that the Founder is not intended to be Booker T. Washington; nor is Ellison's description of the college intended to be a caricature of Tuskegee.

Invisible Man is the story of a Jonah, cursed with the gift of prophecy, cast overboard into the maw of a "white leviathan," vomited up in the streets of a sinful Nineveh. College students do not know much about the Bible these days. Nor should they be expected to recognize Ellison's allusion to the scene at the beginning of *Moby-Dick*, where Ishmael stumbles into a black church with its dismal sermon on the blackness of darkness. Father Mapple's sermon will be equally alien to them, as will Du Bois's use of the term "White Leviathan" in *Dark Princess*, part 1, chapter 3. Nor are they likely to be aware that Ellison has compared his protagonist to Captain Ahab. The student who is particularly interested in Afro-American literature may be interested in the observation that Rudolph Fisher uses the Jonah myth in his short story "The City of Refuge," which appears in *The New Negro* (Locke). Exiting from the subway on his first day in Harlem, Fisher's character is a "Jonah emerging from the whale." Ellison's hero, arriving in New York for the first time, also takes the subway straight to Harlem and emerges feeling like "something regurgitated from the belly of a frantic whale" (156). This, of course, may be coincidence, as may the fact that both Fisher's character and Ellison's hero have the shock of seeing a black policeman directing traffic, immediately after emerging from the whale's belly. But the question of whether there are in this story or elsewhere in Fisher's "Harlem Sketches" any sources or analogues for scenes in *Invisible Man* is a topic for a class discussion rather than a lecture.

Invisible Man is the story of a young man's fight for individuality and personal responsibility. Ellison says in *Shadow and Act* that he considers this a particularly American theme because the "nature of our society is such that we are prevented from knowing who we are" (177). Certainly the Emersonian themes of self-reliance and self-trust have been central to his essays and interviews as well as to his novel. In one of his meditations, the protagonist of *Invisible Man* reflects on Woodridge, his college literature professor, who lectures on Joyce: "Stephen's problem, like ours, was not actually one of creating the uncreated conscience of his race, but of creating the *uncreated features of his face.* . . . We create the race by creating ourselves . . ." (345–46). One of the problems that led to misinterpretations of Ellison by many young black students and writers during the late sixties resulted from having skimmed too hastily the message of Woodridge. When Stephen

Daedalus describes Ireland as the old sow that eats her young, he is issuing a warning against the one-dimensional vision of the nationalist. Ellison's hero, not to mention Ellison himself, is recoiling from one of what Frantz Fanon calls "the pitfalls of national consciousness" (see 119–64). Just as Joyce had to come to grips with Irish nationalism and Thomas Mann had to come to grips with fascism, so too was Ellison forced to an artistic confrontation with the nationalism of Harlem. The typical student, and of course the professor of American literature, will certainly be better equipped to place Ellison's position in context if he or she knows Richard B. Moore's article "Africa Conscious Harlem." I am not suggesting that it is necessary to wade through the voluminous bibliography on black nationalism and Pan-Africanism. Ellison himself does not know it. I do think, however, that knowledge of E. U. Essien-Udom's "Nationalist Movements of Harlem" or Roi Ottley's very readable *New World A-Coming* will be helpful to those who do not know much about black history. I find these useful, because they reveal the nexus between black intellectual life and mass political fantasies. They cover not only Garveyism but several other "Pan-Negro" revivals and awakenings, such as the movement of the 1930s in support of Ras Tafari, the precoronation name of Haile Selassie. It mattered little to the black masses that Garvey held Ras Tafari in profoundest contempt, while the latter ignored the existence of Garvey.

Ellison is doubtless aware of the role that Ethiopia has played in Harlem street-corner mythology and storefront sermons. Like Langston Hughes, he had certainly heard the preachers and soapbox orators prophesying that Ethiopia would stretch forth her hand. The Ethiopian tradition of Africa, America, and the West Indies, as defined by St. Clair Drake, George Shepperson, and others, is certainly important here (see Moses, "Poetics of Ethiopianism," *Black Messiahs*). Ethiopianism is the idea that, as Ellison puts it in the novel, the "world moves in a circle like a roulette wheel. In the beginning, black is on top, in the middle epochs, white holds the odds, but soon Ethiopia shall stretch forth her noble wings! Then place your money on the black!" (80). Ellison's protagonist and the more sophisticated Tod Clifton see only the tip of the iceberg during their confrontation with Ras, and they give it a wide berth, even though they are not aware of its depth and extent in religious and literary experience. The narrator is "glad to be out of the dark and away from that exhorting voice." And Clifton says, "It's a wonder he didn't say something about 'Ethiopia stretching forth her wings' " (367). An interesting topic for a class discussion might be: "Why do Ellison's characters speak of Ethiopia's wings, instead of her hands?" A little effort with a Bible concordance and the aforementioned works might even lead to a good seminar paper.

Ellison has been so emphatic in denying that his novel is derived from a self-contained system of black literary influences and tradition that I think we had better listen to him and believe he means what he is saying. At the same time, we cannot ignore the fact that this book functions in terms of specific references to black institutional life, folklore, and intellectual tradition. It is no accident that Ellison created Dr. Bledsoe around the same time that E. Franklin Frazier was formulating his criticism of black education in *Black Bourgeoisie*. And that was around the same time that Thurgood Marshall was arguing before the Supreme Court that separation in education must inevitably imply inequality. He used a sociological argument based on the work of Frazier and Franklin. We cannot ignore the fact that Ellison wrote about the ambiguous functions of black leadership at the same time that Oliver C. Cox and Ira De A. Reid were making similar statements about black leaders and messiahs. It is not surprising that Ellison created Rinehart within a decade of Arthur Huff Fauset's treatise *Black Gods of the Metropolis*.

Ralph Ellison has never denied that his work is affected by American folklore as well as by European myths and epics, by Popeye the Sailor Man as well as by Ulysses. What has not been much explored is Ellison's early exposure to the depth and complexity of black bourgeois life. He grew up in the proximity of black college communities and had been to Tuskegee. He was and is, as he says in an interview with Stepto and Harper, more sympathetic to black bourgeois intellectuals than Richard Wright was capable of being. Ellison's obsession with individuality of expression is, of course, a characteristic concern of black artists and intellectuals. The tradition of extemporaneous improvisation and solo riffs is no more the property of jazz musicians than it is of highly educated orators like Martin Luther King, Jr.

What Ellison seems to be trying to avoid (and teachers of *Invisible Man* should strive to make this clear) is the reduction of his art to a system of stereotypes and clichés that pass for folklore. In any case, folklore is only a part of black literary tradition in America. There is a tradition of the printed word and a tradition of discussion and debate, centered on the works of Homer and Plato, Shakespeare and Dickens, Washington, Du Bois, and Ayn Rand.

Ellison has also rightly refused to be strapped to the procrustean bed of a naive black aesthetic. Of course it is interesting and useful to know that Ellison discovered and utilized black literary themes such as the Ethiopian tradition. But it is also important to note that, like most other black authors, Ellison is acquainted with the Anglo-American tradition of the New England renaissance. Too often, we seem to forget that Ellison is not the only black author to have read "Civil Disobedience" as well as *Up from Slavery*. To separate Ellison or his work from the world of educated Afro-Americans can be just as misleading as to remove him from the world of blues and folklore.

My suggestion for teaching *Invisible Man* is not that we confine ourselves to lecture. I do, however, think that some systematic lecturing is necessary to make the following points: (1) that *Invisible Man*, like any other book written in English, is part of the numerous traditions that produced it and that it cannot be fully appreciated outside the structure of tradition; (2) that Ralph Ellison grandly asserts his ties to black mass culture and institutional life, which he sees as interwoven with American life as a whole; (3) that the book is not a protest against Tuskegee Institute or even against white racism. It is a story about learning to insist on your individuality and personal responsibility, and on these subjects Ellison has said a lot that needed to be said. After reading *Shadow and Act* and *Going to the Territory* and being introduced to some of the literary and intellectual background, students may begin to wonder whether Ellison has not displayed the same arrogance that many "American scholars" since Emerson have displayed and whether he has always been fully open and honest about acknowledging his intellectual debts, especially to black authors. But that is a question best handled in open classroom discussion.

"Not like an arrow, but a boomerang": Ellison's Existential Blues

Pancho Savery

In teaching *Invisible Man*, I concentrate my efforts on answering two questions: What does the narrator do? How does he do it? What he does is engage in an existential search for his identity, and how he does it is through his recognition of the importance of his folk past, especially the blues. Throughout the novel, the narrator is visited by a series of folk-blues people who attempt to help him understand how to live in the world. Because of his poor education (and by this I don't just mean schooling), the narrator cannot comprehend the importance of these characters and the messages they give him; thus the examples they present go unheeded.

Before I can trace this pattern of visitations, however, I find it necessary to spend some time explaining and defining both existentialism and the blues. I begin by referring to the invisible man's statement "All sickness is not unto death" (14), pointing out to students the reference to Kierkegaard. Students usually have some knowledge of existentialism; and as a basic definition, I give them both Sartre's statement in *Existentialism and Human Emotions* that "existentialism's first move is to make every man aware of what he is and to make the full responsibility of his existence rest on him" (16) and John Fowles's assertion in *The Aristos* that "[e]xistentialism is the revolt of the individual against all those systems of thought, theories of psychology, and social and political pressures that attempt to rob him of his individuality" (122).

I also feel an obligation to go into some detail about the varieties of existentialism; for while Ellison does acknowledge its influence on his work (Hersey 14–17; Geller 159–60; Reed 133), he makes it clear that it is the existentialism of André Malraux, rather than that of Kierkegaard, Sartre, Camus, or Wright, that he found compelling. For Kierkegaard, the "sickness unto death" of the modern world can only be transcended by a blind leap into religion. For Sartre, transcendence comes about through Marxism, which he calls the "untranscendable philosophy for our time" (*Critique* 822). Richard Wright presents for Ellison the same problems as Sartre does because Wright's Marxism and later existentialism are imposed rather than dramatized in his fiction, resulting in what Henri Peyre refers to, introducing a Sartre novel, as "a sociology of literature" (v). For Albert Camus, there is no transcendence. Mersault of *The Stranger* is similar to Bigger Thomas in that they both seem to lack sufficient consciousness of their lives; and both *The Stranger* and *Native Son* seem to fit the description of the naturalistic novel of "final and unrelieved despair" (Ellison, *Shadow* 105) that Ellison is consciously rejecting. Thus, Ellison's version of existentialism rejects the totally negative vision of the world, the lack of consciousness, transcendence, or social responsibility. At the same time, he also rejects transcendence through a specific hierarchy or limited theory, whether politics or religion.

What Ellison accepts is the world of possibility, consciousness, and struggle; the world of ambiguity over the world of cold, predictable logic; in other words, the world of art. This, for Ellison, is the territory of André Malraux. Here, I give students several quotations. In the first, Ellison declares that the artist's task is "to present the human, to make it eloquent, and to provide some sense of transcendence over the given, that is, to make his protest meaningful, significant, and eloquent of human value" (*Going to the Territory* 63). The second quotation comes from Ellison's speculations that Malraux's *Man's Fate* will endure as one of "tomorrow's classics" and that literature, as exemplified by *Man's Fate*, "teaches us more about human choices and the cost of human consciousness" than it does about revolution (Pockell 29). The third quotation is from Malraux's *Voices of Silence*, "All art is a revolt against man's fate" (639).

At this point students usually ask how art is any less of an abstract, logical system than religion or politics, and this provides the transition to the blues. In answer to the question, I begin by citing two statements, the first by Ellison, in which he cautions against propaganda, as opposed to the "brooding, questioning stance that is necessary for fiction" (Hersey 14); and the second by Albert Murray:

> . . . as well meaning as he may be, the truly serious novelist has what almost amounts to an ambivalence toward the human predicament. Alarming as such ambivalence may seem, it is really fundamental to his open-minded search for the essential truth of human experience. (*Omni-Americans* 217–18)

In other words, I tell students, art must be ambiguous precisely because discoveries are made about human nature in the creative act. Propaganda begins with the end point already known. Human life is ambiguous and two-sided, and it seldom if ever conforms to rules or laws. Thus, art, to convey the reality of human existence, must be equally open-ended. The narrator of *Invisible Man*, students need to be reminded, makes his final discoveries about himself through telling us his tale, telling what he did "to be so blue" (14).

Most students either know nothing at all about the blues, associate them only with melancholy, or see them as backward and reactionary. The extensive commentary of both Ellison and Albert Murray (to my mind the single best critic on Ellison, even when, as in *Stomping the Blues*, he never mentions Ellison's name) makes it clear that the blues are something very different and much more. I give my students a handout of quotations on the blues that includes not only Ellison's oft-quoted definition from "Richard Wright's Blues" (*Shadow* 78–79, 94) but also his parenthetical remark in "Change the Joke and Slip the Yoke" on "the innocence of evil and the evil of innocence" expressed in the blues (*Shadow* 53) and his related reference to the blues, in "Remembering Jimmy," as "an art of ambiguity" (*Shadow* 246). Three more quotations complete my presentation on the blues. The first is Ellison's comment in "The World and the Jug" that "the blues transcend the painful conditions with which they deal" (*Shadow* 137). To this I add perhaps the most important statement of all, from Murray:

> André Malraux might well have been referring to the blues and the function of blues musicians when he described the human condition in terms of ever-impending chaos and declared that each victory of the artist represents a triumph of man over his fate. (*Stomping* 42)

The discussion of these quotations should clarify what the blues are and how they serve to transcend the pain of life by turning pain into art; it should also help students understand that the solo blues singer's "autobiographical chronicle" is a struggle to understand the self. Thus, one can refer to the "secular existentialism of the blues," as Ellison does in "As the Spirit Moves Mahalia" (*Shadow* 218).

Just before the narrator's first blues encounter with Louis Armstrong amid his 1,369 light bulbs (1,369 being the square of 37, Ellison's age when he finished the novel in 1951), he tells us to call him "Jack-the-Bear," because he is "in a state of hibernation" (6). While Jack-the-Bear is an allusion to his underground hibernation from which he must emerge, the name of a heroic character from Afro-American folklore ("Out of the Hospital" 247, 263, 277), and the title of a Duke Ellington composition, more important is that Jack-the-Bear was also the nickname of a blues-playing Harlem stride pianist of the 1920s. The narrator is thus clearly identifying himself and his tale as blues-inspired. This connection fits nicely with Murray's description of the novel:

> *Invisible Man* was *par excellence* the literary extension of the blues. It was as if Ellison had taken an everyday twelve bar blues tune (by a man from down South sitting in a manhole up North in New York singing and signifying about how he got there) and scored it for full orchestra. (*Omni-Americans* 239–40)

In a sense, Louis Armstrong is the hero of the novel. He is both the first and the last of the narrator's blues visitors, "the Prometheus of the blues idiom" in Murray's words, whose "assimilation, elaboration, extensions, and refinement of its elements became in effect the touchstone for all who came after him" (*Stomping* 191). The way that Armstrong "bends that military instrument into a beam of lyrical sound" and makes "poetry out of being invisible" (8) serves as a model for the same task that must be undertaken and completed by the narrator. To help students understand how the blues work, I play several recordings throughout my teaching of the novel, beginning, of course, with "(What Did I Do to Be So) Black and Blue," written by Fats Waller for the 1929 musical revue *Connie's Hot Chocolates*. I play two of Armstrong's versions, one from 1929 and one from the late 1950s. The latter is a particularly good example of the dialectical relation between form and content in the blues. Armstrong's soaring, exuberant solos undercut and transcend the total negativity of the lyrics. I also play the 1927 recording of the instrumental "Potato Head Blues," which features Armstrong's famous stop-time solo. Ellison told Robert Stepto and Michael Harper:

> And if Louis Armstrong's meditations on the "Potato Head Blues" aren't marked by elegance, then the term is too inelegant to name the fastidious refinement, the mastery of nuance, the tasteful combination of melody, rhythm, sounding brass and tinkling cymbal which marked his style. (459–60)

"Black and Blue" and "Potato Head Blues" demonstrate that the blues have nothing whatsoever to do with resignation, defeat, and despair. The narrator of *Invisible Man*, however, is not sufficiently aware of this until the end of the novel. When he descends into the depths of "Black and Blue" and journeys through the emotional-historical-personal-religious-mythic levels of Afro-American music and experience, marked by the ambivalence of both the sermon and the slave woman, he cannot understand what he has seen and heard, and he ends up retreating.

It is this blueslike pattern, a lack of complete understanding and retreat, that marks the narrator's encounters with folk-blues characters throughout the novel. It is precisely this pattern that answers the question he asks at the conclusion of the prologue, "But what did *I* do to be so blue?" But until he has sung his own blues song and turned his pain into art, thereby gaining a sense of identity, he will remain in the dark.

The ambiguity-contradiction-boomeranging pattern of the narrator's encounter with the slave woman is repeated in his being haunted by his grandfather's deathbed advice. At the end of the first chapter, after the narrator's humiliation during and after the battle royal, he thinks he has been successful both in making his speech and receiving the scholarship and in extricating himself from the influence of his grandfather's "stolid black peasant's face" (32). When, that night, he dreams of going to the circus and his grandfather laughs at him rather than at the clowns, the narrator should realize that his grandfather's knowledge and experience are superior to his own. But because he believes in the straight line of progress into the future and his grandfather represents the slave past, the narrator blindly goes off to college.

In teaching the section of the novel that concerns the narrator's college career, I concentrate primarily on Jim Trueblood. What is most important for my purposes is Trueblood's connections to the folk-blues tradition. He sings "primitive spirituals" on occasions when "special white guests" visit the college; and the narrator notes that he and the other students are "embarrassed by the earthy harmonies" (46) of Trueblood and his country quartet. Further, he refers to Trueblood's singing as "crude, high, plaintively animal sounds" and notes how everyone at the college hated the "peasants" (46–47). By emphasizing this passage, I stress the link between Trueblood and the grandfather. Both are peasants who have knowledge of and an intimate connection to their folk past, and both are rejected by the narrator. The most important passage in Trueblood's tale comes near the very end:

> I thinks and thinks, until I thinks my brain go'n bust, 'bout how I'm guilty and how I ain't guilty. I don't eat nothin' and I don't drink nothin' and caint sleep at night. Finally, one night, way early in the mornin', I looks up and sees the stars and I starts singin'. I don't mean to, I didn't think 'bout it, just start singin'. I don't know what it was, some kinda church song, I guess. All I know is I *ends up* singin' the blues. I sings me some blues that night ain't never been sang before, and while I'm singin' them blues I makes up my mind that I ain't nobody but myself and ain't nothin' I can do but let whatever is gonna happen, happen. (65–66)

Trueblood is an existential hero who takes control of his life and decides his own fate and destiny. Through the conscious creation of art, specifically by singing the blues and thereby keeping himself in touch with his folk tradition, Trueblood discovers and reaffirms his identity and gains the strength to go on with his life by facing up to his past mistakes and future responsibilities. Like the grandfather and the slave woman, Trueblood is at home with ambiguity and paradox ("how I'm guilty and how I ain't guilty"). And as Ellison says of Bessie Smith in "Richard Wright's Blues," Trueblood sings "lustily as he probes his own grievous wound" (*Shadow* 79). I also connect Trueblood with Louis Armstrong. Trueblood bends the negativity of his life into a form of artistic affirmation as Armstrong bent the notes of his trumpet into the beauty of the blues. Unlike the narrator at the battle royal, who also performs for whites and gets paid, Trueblood is in control of what happens because he is in touch with his folk past and therefore knows who he is. He is nobody but himself, while the narrator is nobody but what others have created.

To further help students understand the blues of this section of the novel,

I play several recordings, beginning with *The Best of Mississippi John Hurt*. This album is especially good because Hurt sings both church songs and blues, as does Jim Trueblood; and as a country-blues artist, Hurt plays the particular kind of blues Trueblood would be most familiar with. In addition, I play selections from side 1 of Hot Tuna's first album, *Hot Tuna*. One of the songs on this album is Leroy Carr's 1928 composition "How Long Blues," a song that Ellison specifically labels "existentialist" (Geller 167). The lyrics (Hughes and Bontemps 396–97) begin by expressing a typical blues sentiment, sorrow over lost love. The singer feels sorry for himself because his baby's left him, and he knows neither where she's gone nor when (if ever) she'll return. By the end of the song, however, he has decided that he cannot wait forever and that if some day she returns to apologize, he will have been long gone. This is also the song the narrator hears Jack-the-Bear sing in Ellison's "Out of the Hospital and under the Bar" (277).

Students should, by now, be clear about the ongoing pattern. The narrator encounters those who know who they are, who are in touch with their traditions, and who attempt to give him good advice. He consistently rejects, doesn't understand, or fails to follow through on the examples presented. Rather, he heeds the advice of those who are blind to their traditions or who want the narrator to follow in their footsteps instead of creating his own. The vet, who while in France forgot some things "most peasants and folk people almost always know through experience" (89) and who tells the narrator he is invisible (92), is rejected for Norton, "teller of polite Negro stories" (37) and defender of the Founder. Likewise, Miss Susie Gresham, whose presence causes the narrator to erupt into spontaneous blues-jazz language, is forgotten for the blind Homer Barbee and Herbert Bledsoe of the fake leg iron, both also defenders of the Founder's veiled vision.

Paralleling the narrator's move from the South to the North, his first blues encounter in New York is with an exemplar of the city, rather than country, blues. While pushing a shopping cart full of blueprints, Peter Wheatstraw (named for the blues singer Peetie Wheatstraw [1902–41], who, like the character in the novel, was known as the "Devil's Son-in-Law") sings a verse from the Count Basie and Jimmy Rushing blues "Boogie Woogie," which I play in class. When the narrator hears the song, he tells us that "some memories slipped around my life at the campus and went far back to things I had long ago shut out of my mind" (169–70). Wheatstraw is here linked with Trueblood, as representing a living folk-blues sensibility that the college has attempted to stamp out. The narrator has forgotten the correct response to the folk question "[I]s you got the dog?" (170). Furthermore, he has difficulty with the ambiguous, contradictory, blues-toned language of Wheatstraw. The narrator, rather than Wheatstraw, is the believer in plans, blueprints, and organized, logical, "scientific" thought. Wheatstraw's cart full of unused plans should be a sign to the narrator that this is not the way the world works. The narrator's final comment, "God damn . . . they're a hell of a people!" (174), indicates his distance from and lack of identification with the folk past represented by Wheatstraw (as well as by the slave woman, his grandfather, Trueblood, the vet, and Susie Gresham) and connects him to the school officials who referred to the blacks' "primitive spirituals." Immediately after this conversation, thinking that a counterman has committed a racial slur in suggesting pork chops and grits to him, he feels proud that he resisted the dish as "an act of discipline" (175). When the narrator sees the same offer made to a white man, he realizes his mistake; but by then, it is too late. This scene makes a nice contrast to the yam scene later on, when the narrator is less reluctant to eat soul food but is still naive in believing it will solve all his problems.

The next blues character I focus on is Mary Rambo. Students inevitably complain about the paucity of fully developed female characters. And while I agree with this criticism, I also give students Ellison's introduction to "Out of the Hospital and under the Bar" (243–44), in which he explains his original plan of having Mary release the narrator from the machine at the paint-factory hospital. Even without this explanation, however, Mary is clearly another positive folk-blues character in the narrator's life. In class I emphasize her care for the narrator, her role in the community, the way she makes the narrator think of the blues (producing "a feeling of old, almost forgotten relief" [247]), her quoting of Mahalia Jackson (249), and her singing (290) of the Bessie Smith classic "Back Water Blues," which inspires the narrator to attempt to find a job. I play the Bessie Smith song, and I note Mary's blues-toned contradictory language. Her comment "I'm in New York but New York ain't in me" (249) not only echoes Peter Wheatstraw's contradictory comments on Harlem's being both a bear's den and the best place to be (171) but is also a direct quote from a railroad porter Ellison interviewed in 1939 for the Federal Writers Project (Siskind 54). Another example occurs when the narrator is attempting to pay Mary his back rent after he has joined the Brotherhood, while she is more concerned about the bitter taste of the morning coffee:

> "Guess I'll have to get better filters," she mused. "These I got just lets through the grounds along with the coffee, the good with the bad. I don't know though, even with the best of filters you apt to find a ground or two at the bottom of your cup." (315)

More than any other passage in the novel, this statement conveys the ambiguity or dialectic of the blues and demonstrates that the world moves "not like an arrow, but a boomerang" (6).

Unfortunately, the narrator continues to believe that he can remove the contradiction from the world and have it proceed along a straight line. Like Wheatstraw (169–70) and Mary (252), the yam man (256, 258) reminds the narrator of a part of his past he has forgotten. And while the narrator has progressed to a point where he is no longer embarrassed to be seen eating soul food, he thinks that such a breakthrough is all it takes to reclaim his identity: "I yam what I am!" (260). But the yam seller reminds him that "everything what looks good ain't necessarily good" (258), and, indeed, the narrator finds that one of the yams is frostbitten. When he walks down the street and encounters Primus Provo and his wife, the narrator feels drawn to them and experiences "strange memories awakening" (264). Their evicted possessions, including old blues records, represent both their personal history and a kind of collective history of Afro-Americans that causes the narrator to identify with them, think of his mother, and finally make a speech on their behalf. His identification is short-lived, however, when he accepts Brother Jack's "scientific" assessment that the Provos are "agrarian types" and "individuals" who "don't count" (284) and agrees to his suggestion that the narrator forget his past, cease communicating with his family, and leave Mary's to seek a new name and identity.

By this point of the novel, if not earlier, students are usually having fun. They easily recognize the various manipulations of the Brotherhood and can connect them to those of the men at the battle royal and to Bledsoe, Brockway, Kimbro, Emerson, and Norton. This part of *Invisible Man* can be taught very quickly, except when I pause for Brother Tarp and Tod Clifton's funeral. Tarp is one of the few members of the Brotherhood who likes the narrator's arena speech, despite its lapse into the unscientific personal realm (336–37). Tarp is also important because his gift of the portrait of Frederick Douglass is in contrast to Brother Jack's desire to make the narrator "the new Booker T. Washington, but even greater than he" (300). After receiving the gift, the narrator stares at the portrait, "feeling a sudden piety, remembering and refusing to hear the echoes of my grandfather's voice" (370). And after reading Brother Jack's anonymous letter, he calls Tarp into his office and sees his grandfather looking from Tarp's eyes. Here I connect Jack and Bledsoe as the writers of dubious letters and connect them both to the dream the narrator has the night of the battle royal. Although students are often confused about the meaning of the grandfather, connecting him to Tarp at least makes it clear that the narrator is not correctly following the grandfather's advice. This becomes more clear when we discuss Tarp's story of his life on the chain gang, his gift of the link to the narrator, the contrast between this link and the one on Bledsoe's desk, and Tarp's final desertion from the Brotherhood (and his removal of the Douglass portrait) when it changes tactics.

It is in this context that I also discuss Tod Clifton. He leaves the Brotherhood at the same time and for the same reason that Tarp does, because the Brotherhood has shelved the "old techniques of agitation" (418) that were Douglass's trademark. The difference between Tarp and Clifton is that Tarp still has his sense of personal and racial history and identity to fall back on as a source of strength. Clifton had given up everything for the Brotherhood. When it fails him, he has nothing left and ends up on the street corner selling Sambo dolls. Both the turnout for Tod Clifton's funeral and the passage in which the narrator describes the baritone-horn duet on "No More Auction Block" ("There's Many a Thousand Gone") show that there is and was a tradition for Clifton to fall back on, a tradition that obviously sustained Tarp. As with every other potential moment of folk-blues recognition in the novel, the narrator fails to grasp the implications. He remains with the Brotherhood even though they reduce Clifton to a type—"Brutus," "traitor" (454, 456)—just as they had similarly reduced Primus Provo and his wife. He even stays after he discovers Jack's blindness, which connects Jack with Barbee, Bledsoe, the Founder, and Norton. The narrator's being mistaken for Rinehart, his understanding of Rinehart's significance in the community, and his realization, through Rinehart, that he is invisible should have been all he needed to leave the Brotherhood. Instead, he decides "to do a Rinehart" (496) in order to subvert the Brotherhood, thinking that he has finally understood and is following his grandfather's deathbed advice. But Rinehart (named after a nineteenth-century Harvard undergraduate sung about by Jimmy Rushing in "Harvard Blues," by Count Basie) is not the right model to follow; he is "an opportunist" (Geller 159) and "the personification of chaos" (*Shadow* 181). Although he knows who he is, he is an anarchist with no social responsibility. The narrator's dehumanizing affair with Sybil and his responsibility for the riot are proof of this. And finally, the actions of Dupre during the riot reveal that the Brotherhood has nothing to offer and that the narrator has been misinterpreting events and following the wrong advice his entire life.

Only in the epilogue, after the narrator has told his story to himself and to us, his readers, and spent a sufficient amount of time in hibernation, does he understand his grandfather's advice. My teaching of the epilogue concentrates on the narrator's finally grasping his grandfather's meaning, which he realizes he has got all wrong. What it comes down to is seeing the inherent contradictions in American life and understanding that contradiction is the way of the world. Furthermore, he recognizes that he, as an individual, must take personal responsibility for the principles of American democracy. Only when he creates "the *uncreated features of his face*" (346), gives birth to himself as a conscious individual, uses his imagination to create art rather than to remain in the chaos of a Rinehart or the rootlessness of a Tod Clifton, and continues "to play in face of certain defeat" (564), can he hope to succeed.

I end my teaching of the novel by playing three versions of "Buddy

Bolden's Blues" (one by the composer, Jelly Roll Morton, and two by Armstrong), from which comes the line "Open the window and let the foul air out" (567). I do this for three reasons. First, the mention of Louis Armstrong allows me to make the novel come full circle (or boomerang). Second, the narrator's comments on Armstrong and the line from the song demonstrate finally that the narrator has learned not only to live with but to relish the contradiction and ambiguity of life, or what Ellison refers to in "That Same Pain, That Same Pleasure" as "the mixture of the marvelous and the terrific" (*Shadow* 20). Finally, the song gives me the opportunity once again to make sure that students understand how *Invisible Man* is a blues novel and to connect the workings of the blues to the novel's last line. To do this, I use several quotations. The first is from Onwuchekwa Jemie:

> But the life whose story is told may not be the singer's. Indeed, it may not be one life at all but a composite of lives; for like any gifted artist, the blues singer is able to enter into the lives of others, to draw into his song their experiences, problems, emotions, and moods and to render these as though they were his own.   (43)

To this I add a passage by Janheinz Jahn:

> For the blues singer does not in fact express *his* personal experiences and transfer them to his audience; on the contrary, it is the experiences of the community that he is expressing, making himself its spokesman. . . . it is not the personal experience that is emphasized, but the typical experience.   (223)

In using these quotations, I am attempting to stress the relation between the blues singer and the community he or she sings to and for. This sense of involvement with others makes *Invisible Man* a profoundly political novel. "It's just that," as Larry Neal says, "Ellison's politics are ritualistic as opposed to secular" (Hersey 79). In other words, to quote Neal again, "even though the blues are cast in highly personal terms, they stand for the collective sensibility of a people at particular stages of cultural, social, and political development" ("Ethos" 46). Thus, by emphasizing the existential blues elements of the novel, I try to help students see not only how both Ellison and the narrator have made sense of their personal lives and their relationships to the world around them but that this same process of self-discovery and commitment must take place in students' own lives outside the classroom as well.

Ellison's Narrator as Emersonian Scholar

Eleanor Lyons

Like many readers of *Invisible Man*, my students tend not to see that it moves beyond an indictment of society to expose the narrator's complicity in the events that drive him underground or, as Ellison once put it, his "refusal to run the risk of his own humanity, which involves guilt" (*Shadow* 179). Nor are they comfortable with his decision to rejoin society and explore the "possibility that even an invisible man has a socially responsible role to play" (568). By approaching the novel in terms of Emersonian self-reliance, however, I can help counter this tendency to misunderstand exactly what's gone wrong for the narrator and how he plans to try and put it right. In some cases this means providing the Emersonian context myself, but in American literature classes I assign "The American Scholar" in conjunction with the novel and base discussion on parallels between the two works. Although the extent to which I pursue specific parallels might vary considerably from one group to another, I want students to see that the narrator finally emerges as the Emersonian scholar whose duty, despite the sobering ironies in any such statement, is "to cheer, to raise, and to guide men by showing them facts amidst appearances" (100). Discussion should, in other words, make students realize that Ellison portrays an Emersonian affirmation of self and life not only as feasible in our twentieth-century context but also as necessary for reform.

We spend some time at the outset on issues raised in the prologue, with particular emphasis on the narrator's determination to blame his invisibility solely on society; his boomerang theory of history; and the Louis Armstrong refrain "What did I do to be so black and blue?" Although students aren't usually prepared at this point to respond in any depth to my question about whether the narrator's attitude or his understanding of events subsequently changes, I raise it in preparation for discussion of the epilogue. Moving on to his academic career, I emphasize that what he did—in answer to that nagging blues refrain in the prologue—was run from the Emersonian self-reliance that would have enabled him to fulfill his obligations to himself and society. After establishing this direction in the smoker episode, we can discuss his experience at college as a twentieth-century counterpart to the educational scene Emerson so roundly condemns in "The American Scholar." Students can see for themselves how the training that should according to Emersonian ideals inspire the narrator to shape his own truths and be his own hero has instead instilled in him, and others like him, a blind dedication to the Founder, effectively reducing them to what Emerson calls "men . . . of no account" (106). In addition, Bledsoe takes his place beside the academic leaders Emerson censured a hundred and fifty years ago for capitulating to the materialism of the times rather than insisting on the courage and vision that might improve conditions. Before concluding this discussion, however, I stress that the failures of the educational system, and of the white society behind it, in no way exonerate the narrator from the sacrifice of self we have been talking about.

Events in New York shed further light on his unwitting but determined effort to avoid the kind of education Emerson advocates, which is not so much a matter of formal training as it is the ongoing adventure of self-realization. Students must first understand that the Emersonian scholar is the individual who shapes experience into an increasingly accurate account of the self in accord with the natural law of development called "polarity." "The mind now thinks, now acts," as Emerson explains, each new action or experience generating a more comprehensive insight into self and life, which in turn demands expression (99). It is important to emphasize, though, that circumstances represent or bespeak the individual only insofar as he or she does act on this understanding instead of subordinating it to external authority of any sort. Once this is clear, students can discuss the narrator's invisibility as the result of a refusal to confront the truth events would teach him. By this time, actually, most of the class seem quite comfortable with the distinction between society's unwillingness to acknowledge his individuality and his own failure to discover and insist upon it. They are also prepared to discuss the suggestion that he is shunted back and forth by events in a pattern of retreat described by his own boomerang theory rather than by Emersonian polarity, until flight finally throws him back unconditionally on the self he has worked so hard to deny.

Since a number of students have some difficulty understanding that the narrator runs as well from his own awareness of this self-betrayal, I underscore evidence that the "grandfather part" of him has known his motives—and objected—all along. In the discussion of events in New York, for example, I spend a good deal of time on the episode in the factory hospital, urging everyone to notice how the narrator's inability to remember his name brings him perilously close to the realization that he himself might be responsible for the problem he is having with his identity. As he puts it, "I suspected that I was really playing a game with myself and that they were taking part" (237). The twentieth-century businessman named Emerson also tends to be confusing for students, but that confusion clears up when we look at him and his son as products of America's refusal to hear the nineteenth-century challenge of self-reliance except in terms of economic gain. Nor does Rinehart seem quite so enigmatic once students recognize him as the individual who in Emersonian terms has so thoroughly violated the integrity of his being that he assumes the contours of his situation, which means that he epitomizes the concept of invisibility. I like to clarify this point by asking them to compare Rinehart with Tod Clifton, whose compelling honesty enables him to shape from the circumstances of defeat a statement of who he is.

When we move to the narrator's account of being driven underground and refusing to run any further, discussion centers on the Emersonian adventure of self-realization that finally gets under way. Once I establish a link between the narrator's burning of those papers in his briefcase and the scholar's use of the past as "raw material" for the present, students can deal effectively with the suggestion that this twentieth-century protagonist has, as Emerson says of his contemporaries, not only "wronged himself" but "almost lost the light that can lead him back to his prerogatives" (106). The point, of course, is that the narrator does manage, with the aid of those 1,369 light bulbs, to see in all that has happened the "prerogatives" of a manhood or a "wholeness" only he can violate. Students can also discuss in some depth the way in which he is finally governed by Emerson's concept of polarity, gaining from his experiences an insight into himself and twentieth-century society that he then acts on by shaping it into a work of art or a public statement of who he is. And this brings us to the question I'd raised earlier about the possibility that the epilogue reveals some significant changes in his attitude. I introduce that question here by asking whether the act of telling his story concludes the narrator's self-realization or, rather, provides him with more information, more "raw material," to be understood and expressed.

Students must first remember that the epilogue follows from the narrator's decision to set other matters aside and, as he puts it, "try belatedly to study the lesson of my own life" (559). With that in mind, they have little difficulty understanding that he hears the evidence against himself in the story he has just told and finally acknowledges the extent to which cowardice and conformity have made him party to his oppression. The action suggested by this new insight makes sense to them as they recognize the Emersonian affirmation in it and see that what in fact the narrator intends to do is emerge from his underground hole and assume the burden of the one freedom that can't be denied him: the freedom to insist, whatever the cost, on the integrity of his being. But the full significance of this affirmation becomes clear only as students pursue the idea that self-reliance enables him to fulfill, in addition to the primary obligation to himself, the "socially responsible role" that has been his goal from the outset (568). Discussion should reveal, in other words, that Ellison's novel works exactly as the Emerson essay does, setting against a condemnation of existing conditions the hope that they can and will improve through action of the sort contemplated by the narrator.

With an understanding of the role Emerson envisions for his scholar, students are in an excellent position to see that the narrator, too, serves as a reminder of moral "prerogatives" that have been largely forgotten—but not entirely lost—in the dedication to power and position that continues to characterize American society. While they are under no illusions about his predicament as a black man, they realize that by maintaining his own stature he can continue the task he has in fact already begun, helping to restore the priorities and inspire the changes in attitude that lead, in turn, to the possibility of reform. For Ellison's account of this Emersonian aim and its importance to the American novel, we look at "Brave Words for a Startling Occasion" (*Shadow*). I generally conclude with the suggestion, if students haven't already made it themselves, that such are the "facts" enabling the narrator, exactly as Emerson says the scholar must, "to cheer, to raise, and to guide" his contemporaries.

"An American Negro Idiom":
Invisible Man and the Politics of Culture

Cushing Strout

Stendhal's remark about politics in a novel being like the sound of a pistol shot at a concert reflects a common critical prejudice. It is a prejudice alien to literary treatment of the race problem, however, for historically in America the legacy of slavery in a nation with democratic ideals has inevitably given a political dimension to the dramatization of race relations. The gap between ideal and actual has made the figure of invisibility for the black's identity a recurrent one in works ranging from Melville's *Benito Cereno* to Richard Wright's *Native Son*, two influential literary ancestors of Ralph Ellison's *Invisible Man*, as Todd M. Lieber has noted. Issues of politics, history, and culture always converge in any profound analysis of the race problem, whatever the medium. No one proves the point better than Ellison in his essays, interviews, and fiction. His example is especially telling because, as he made clear in vigorous debate with Irving Howe, the black writer is "no mere product of his socio-political predicament" (*Shadow* 112). Ellison is deeply devoted to his craft as a novelist, but he also insists that literature has taught him something about his "identity as Western man, as political being" (*Shadow* 117). By the markers of these balanced assertions, Ellison has charted his own channel as a novelist.

To grasp the politics of culture in Ellison's novel is to see its kinship to his essays and interviews, especially those collected in *Shadow and Act* and *Going to the Territory*. Ellison's subtlety has often escaped his critics, whether black or white, and his sharp and independent observations on the race problem have often been out of step with fashionable political tendencies. In 1968, for example, a *Negro Digest* poll of forty black writers elected Richard Wright to first place and relegated Ellison to fourth. Donald B. Gibson reflected such a view when he described Ellison as a "personal and subjective" writer "who denies his relation to the group of black people" by an individualism that gives up on the racial problem and asserts that "the best that can be done" is to "withdraw into the inner recesses of our own psyches" (309). But Larry Neal, who had once led the attack on Ellison and then reversed himself, celebrated *Invisible Man* as one of "the world's most successful 'political novels' " (79).

Students can better keep political themes in *Invisible Man* in mind if they pay close attention to the ideas Ellison has elaborated elsewhere about the black experience in American history. For example, in a course Fiction and Democracy at New York University and in his speech accepting the National Book Award, he defined the essence of his novel as an experimental attempt "to return to the mood of personal moral responsibility for democracy which typified the best of our nineteenth-century fiction" (*Shadow* 102).

Invisible Man has generated metaphysical, psychological, existential, symbolist, and folkloristic readings—all of which have their basis not only in critical fashions but in the fecundity of the novel's linguistic energy. It is important, nevertheless, to emphasize that Ellison sees the novel form as being "bound up with the notion of nationhood" and dealing with "the impact of change upon personality" (*Going* 242, 244). Interpreters seeking myths and archetypes in Ellison's fiction can easily find them, but he warns that "novels are time-haunted" and that, if its symbols link up with those of myth, "they do so by virtue of their emergence from the specific texture of a specified form of social reality" (*Shadow* 57). For Ellison's novel, anyway, it is crucial to recognize that the "moral imperatives of American life" are historically implicit in the Declaration of Independence, the Constitution, and the Bill of Rights. These ideals measure the black's progress and make the black a test for democracy's morale. As Ellison affirms, "In the beginning was not only the word but the contradiction of the word" (*Going* 243).

Ellison has revealed that as a boy he once assisted his "adopted grandfather" (*Shadow* 155), the black custodian of Oklahoma's State Law Library and a man very knowledgeable about the law he was then not allowed to participate in making. Later Ellison noted that he grew up to believe that "the Constitution is a script, by which we seek to act out the drama of democracy and the stage upon which we enact our roles" (*Going* 330).

In considering Ellison's indebtedness to some of the legal bases for America's democratic system, my classes focus on how literature, like law, creates symbolic forms of order, but how the novelist, being able to socialize "emotions and interest held in check" by manners and laws, can raise to consciousness the cultural tendency of psychological projection, "this identification of the socially unacceptable with the blacks" (*Going* 329, 338). In this regard, it is also important for students to know that, having once clerked for the influential psychiatrist Harry Stack Sullivan, Ellison brings to his work an acute psychological awareness of how Freudian defense mechanisms pertain to an understanding of the racial problem. Indeed, his novel is a kind of psychohistory, but it is staged within the political framework of the democratic drama.

Students need to recognize too that just as Ishmael is not Melville and Huck Finn is not Mark Twain, so the invisible man is not Ellison. Rather, the narrating "I" is a nameless vernacular voice, representing a career that symbolizes the major stages of the black experience in America. But it is helpful for students to see that elements of Ellison's past do orient the book's perspective: the memory of his grandfather, who confronted a mob that had formed to lynch a friend; his education as a music major at Tuskegee Institute in segregated Alabama; his role as reviewer for the *New Masses* (1937–40) and as managing editor for the *Negro Quarterly* (1942); his collecting of folklore for the Federal Writers Project (1938–42); his report of a Harlem riot for the *New York Post* (2 Aug. 1943); and his joining of the Merchant Marine in World War II as a protest against a Jim Crow army.

The narrator of *Invisible Man* is always guided by his slave grandfather's advice, "Agree 'em to death and destruction" (16). Yet he comes to understand his grandfather's political meaning only in the epilogue, only after he has suffered a long experience of misinterpreting the advice. Indeed, throughout the body of the novel, instead of asserting his own independent judgment, he internalizes the expectations of others. This theme recurs with variations, like a jazz riff played on Ellison's trumpet, as a form of the blues, emanating from an underground man, whose position echoes Ellison's reading of Dostoevsky and Richard Wright. The narrator's retrospective story moves from slavery to Reconstruction by focusing on one of Reconstruction's institutions, a black college, run on paternalistic lines, not unlike Tuskegee Institute. Such colleges were inspired by Booker T. Washington's conservative doctrine of separate-but-equal development, a position ratified by the Supreme Court in *Plessy v. Ferguson* (1896) when it sanctioned racial segregation on railroads.

Once again, the novel takes on new meaning for students when they are offered additional autobiographical context. For example, the novel moves the narrator north to the Harlem of the depression of the 1930s, where Ellison himself had moved in 1936. As editor of the *Negro Quarterly*, irritated by the patronizing paternalism of leftists, Ellison invoked the symbol of the zoot suit (cited later by Larry Neal) for its possible "profound political meanings" as a reminder that the masses must be "helped to see the bright star of their hopes through the fog of their daily experiences" by "a Negro leadership that is aware of the psychological attitude and incipient forms of action which the black masses reveal in their emotion-charged myths, symbols and wartime folklore" ("Editorial"). A decade later the novelist dramatized the same point when the narrator reflects that the three zoot-suited young blacks on the subway platform with him are men "outside of historical time," as the Marxist Brotherhood measures it, yet they might be "the true leaders, the bearers of something precious" if history were, after all, not "a force in a laboratory experiment," but "a gambler" with an ace in the hole, "a madman full of paranoid guile and these boys his agents, his big surprise!" (430–31). The Brotherhood Marxists would consider the three boys *lumpenproletariat*, unfit for the revolution, but—by the light of Ellison's nonrational historicism—the narrator, despite his membership in the Brotherhood, sees them differently, trembling with the thought of the potentiality of these migrants "who shoot up from the South into the busy city like wild jacks-in-the-box" (429).

The promise of these men "outside history" seems to be redeemed in the novel when the invisible man exults at the riot for expressing the blacks' powers of self-determination: "They organized it and carried it through alone; the decision their own and their own action. Capable of their own action . . ." (536). His enthusiasm, anticipatory of later black ideologies of self-determination, is short-lived, however, because he discovers that the rebels have been exploited by the Brotherhood committee that had planned the riot: "And I had helped, had been a tool. . . . By pretending to agree I *had* indeed agreed, had made myself responsible for that huddled form lighted by flame and gunfire in the street, and all the others whom now the night was making ripe for death" (541). Only then does he realize that the brothers "want the streets to flow with blood" so that they can turn "death and sorrow and defeat into propaganda" (545). Bitter at the Brotherhood's resentment of his independent efforts to arouse the masses, recognizing the blindness of Marxist class categories to his ethnicity, and smarting from Marxist disdain for his "old agrarian self," the narrator concludes that the Brotherhood's dream of bringing "both science and history under control" is a rationalistic delusion.

As the Communist party in the 1930s had done for many Harlem Negroes, the Brotherhood had first offered the invisible man "the possibility of being more than a member of a race" (346). In giving his arena speech, the invisible man believed he had become "more human" through his Brotherhood experience (337). In the epilogue, however, he recollects that his grandfather, though a slave, had "never had any doubts about his humanity" but had accepted it just as "he accepted the principle" of equality that "lives on in all its human and absurd diversity" (567). This disillusionment with the Brotherhood parallels the experience of many Harlem intellectuals with the Communist party, even though the party had played an important role in mobilizing the defense of the Scottsboro boys, who were accused of rape and whom Ellison had also supported in their struggle for justice. The party incongruously joined the ideas of ethnic "self-determination of the Black Belt" and class struggle; and Eugene Gordon, a speaker at the American Writers' Congress in 1935, treated black folklore and music as a "national psychosis" resulting from repression (143). The party later supported segregated armed forces, and it subordinated black reform to the Soviets' Popular Front strategy in the war. This expediency is reflected in the novel's portrait of the riot.

The novel's black nationalist, Ras the Destroyer, recognizes the importance of ethnicity to identity, and his back-to-Africa theme is historically linked to Marcus Garvey's mass movement of the 1920s. But Ras is an anachronistic warrior with a spear. The next step in the narrator's education belongs to the protean Rinehart. Behind his dark glasses, Rinehart is a preacher, lover, and numbers racketeer. The trickster is a venerable figure in black folklore; and for Ellison, Rinehart's shrewd sense of role changing effectively transforms the Marxist idea of freedom as "the recognition of necessity" into the pluralist idea of freedom as "the recognition of possibility" (488). It is in this sense that Rinehart's glasses are "a political instrument" for the narrator, teaching him what he cannot learn from either Marxism or black nationalism.

Ellison's criticism of the Left is not from the Right, as some 1940s essays prove. In 1944, reviewing Gunnar Myrdal's *American Dilemma*, Ellison dismissed the New Deal point of view "as the eclectic creation of a capitalism in momentary retreat" and insisted on the reality of "an American class struggle" (*Shadow* 310–11, 315). Yet he faulted the Socialist Myrdal for interpreting black cultural manifestations as merely "secondary reactions to more primary pressures from the side of the 'dominant white majority' " instead of seeing them as possibly embodying "a *rejection* of what [Myrdal] considers 'higher values' " (315). Why cannot blacks, Ellison asked in a memorable phrase, "have made a life upon the horns of the white man's dilemma?" (316). From this point of view slavery was not merely victimization, as recent historians have demonstrated, and the invisible man's grandfather did not need the Marxist Brotherhood to become human.

Ellison's 1948 essay "Harlem Is Nowhere" (*Shadow*) is remarkably prophetic of the dreamlike texture of the novel's Harlem riot and provides a valuable clue to the factory hospital scene, which often puzzles students. The essay describes the Lefargue Clinic, Harlem's only psychiatric institution, as an "attempt to provide psychotherapy for the underprivileged"; hence it is for Ellison an "underground extension of democracy" (295). Harlem in this essay is like "the distorted images that appear in dreams," quivering with "hidden and threatening significance" (296). Ellison focuses on Harlem's psychological character—"a character that arises from the impact between urban slum conditions and folk sensibilities" (296)—to define the process of change that swept American blacks from slavery to industrialism in eighty-five years. History thus generated a world "so fluid and shifting that often within the mind the real and unreal merge, and the marvelous beckons from behind the same sordid reality that denies its existence" (297). It is this frustrating surreal world that produced the Harlem riots of 1935 and 1943, Ellison asserts, because the great migration northward cut the black man off from his "peasant cynicism," his sense of being "at home in the world," his "authoritative religion which gives his life a semblance of metaphysical wholeness," a stable family structure, and "a body of folklore—tested in life-and-death terms against his daily experience with nature and the Southern white man—that serves him as a guide to action" (298, 299).

In the factory hospital scene, Ellison condenses this idea of culture shock.

Connected to an electrical machine that in effect lobotomizes without surgery, the narrator experiences a new birth after his journey from South to North. Listening to his doctors, he imagines that they are engaged in "a discussion of history" (231). "Harlem Is Nowhere" has prepared us for understanding this symbolic scene. The shock treatment produces amnesia in the narrator—except for a remnant of children's folklore about the tricksters Buckeye and Brer Rabbit. This surviving link to his black southern identity is crucial, however, in maintaining the continuity in his search for freedom. This identity is nurtured later by the caretaking of Mary Rambo, who rehabilitates him after the bewildering trauma of the machine and of the hostility of both foreman and union leaders in the paint factory. She reminds him, that "It's the ones from the South"—the ones who "knows the fire and ain't forgot how it burns"—who will take the lead in moving the race "on up a little higher" because they won't "forgits the ones on the bottom" (249).

In the end, the narrator realizes that he cannot go home again, not to Mary's, the campus, or the Brotherhood. Reading the epilogue, students now see that he will emerge from underground if only because he has to do so to write his memoir. Still, for many students the "socially responsible role" of the invisible man seems too obscure. Ellison has spoken of his hero as having changed from "a rabble-rouser" to a writer, but for Ellison protest is an element in all art, which itself is a social act, as he made clear in his debate with Irving Howe. Moreover, the epilogue resonates with his 1958 interview "Some Questions and Some Answers" (*Shadow*), which is the best place to appreciate his politics of culture in defining black identity. There he sees the American Negro as basically Protestant in religion, Western in kinship system, and American in historical sense and secular values. Yet there are "an American Negro idiom, style, and way of life" (271) interacting with the larger body of American culture. For Ellison, "it is not culture which binds the peoples who are of partially African origin now scattered throughout the world, but an identity of passions" (263), a common hatred of colonization, which is a matter of political, not cultural, potency. For himself, Ellison defines his task as "trying to communicate, to articulate and define a group experience" (267) that influences and is influenced by American values.

This complex position was never congenial to black nationalists of the 1960s, who envisioned an autonomous black culture and a future black nation. From their perspective Ellison, by making art transcendent, has "constructed for himself a refuge from the demands of black liberation," as Houston A. Baker, Jr., put it (*Journey* 118). But the crucial point is in the autobiographical "Hidden Name and Complex Fate" (*Shadow*), where Ellison connects the artist's development of technique to the discovery of "values which turn in their *own* way" (163) on the central issues affecting one's nation and time. For him the American novelist must always bear the burden of the ideals enshrined in "the sacred papers" of the founders. "Responsibility rests upon recognition, and recognition is a form of agreement," the invisible man observes in the prologue (14), commenting on the white man who had bumped into and insulted him without ever really having seen him. In the epilogue a circle is completed—like the throw of a boomerang—when Mr. Norton, the white trustee of the black college, symbolically and actually fails to recognize the narrator, the former student he had once known.

Only in the nation's political response to the civil rights movement of the 1960s did public awareness of the newly visible blacks lead to some social agreement on liberty and equality, those principles the narrator's grandfather had represented as the only sure basis for black identity. Far from being empty rhetoric, the epilogue in its form, as John F. Callahan points out, is "an advance on the tradition of first person American novels because it implies a continuing responsibility on the part of the narrator for his story" ("Democracy" 67) as he shoulders the burden of summing up its point and bearing. The narrator's "pursuit of happiness" has at last taken him back to the implicit promise of Jefferson's Declaration, the grand manifesto of a statesman whose noble house, as Ellison has remarked, was built by his slaves.

Ellison has a strong sense of his affiliation to the classic American writers. Like them, he works with a technique of symbolism, and his novel dramatizes a journey of growth. In these respects its hero has some affinity with Melville's Ishmael and Twain's Huck, but the invisible man's journey is not his alone. It reflects the various stages of black history in America, and so it provides the perspective of what Ellison calls "a Negro American idiom" on our society and culture.

Ultimately, then, *Invisible Man* does dramatize the traditional idea of an American pilgrimage, but it does so on its own terms. It satirizes what it calls "the black rite of Horatio Alger" (109) in the visiting millionaires' speeches at the narrator's college; it undercuts any linear notion of progress by seeing history as analogous to a boomerang in its trajectory; and it reveals the narrator's journey to be a series of illusions from which he is recurringly disenthralled. The epilogue classically evokes the traditional myth of America as possibility and as equality, yet it links them to an ideal of diversity and rejects conformity to dominant color or opinion in a country historically "woven of many strands" (564). Far from seeking refuge in aesthetic individualism, as its detractors have charged, Ellison's novel looks to politics and history for the fulfillment of its narrator's identity. Ellison puts an existentialist's emphasis on knowing who one is as a condition for freedom, but for him that discovery is not only personal but communal. He is an existentialist in the terms of Malraux rather than of Sartre. In this respect the invisible man not only foreshadows the future; in the civil rights movement of the 1960s he had one.

Losing It "even as he finds it": The Invisible Man's Search for Identity

Christopher Sten

No other American novelist has been so obsessed with the search for identity as Ralph Ellison has. It is, he has said in *Shadow and Act,* "*the* American theme" (177). Yet no other American novelist has seemed to find the search so inconclusive, or treated the subject with a more profound sense of irony, taking away with one hand what he seems to bestow with the other. Thus as a novel about the modern hero's search for identity—particularly the black man's struggle for visibility and wholeness in America in the period between the depression and the early years of World War II—Ellison's *Invisible Man* presents the teacher with a formidable challenge. It portrays the nameless title character in a series of disillusioning episodes wherein the identity he thought he was constructing is repeatedly stripped from him, leaving him not only naked but "invisible." In the end, living in an underground coal bin in New York, where he finally comes to accept his invisibility, he appears to have nothing, to have acquired no "positive" identity whatsoever; he seems not to have achieved the vital sense of self that permits one to function productively in the world of everyday affairs. Except in the epilogue, where he proclaims his faith that he will one day end his hibernation and return to the upper world, there to assert himself once again—an expression of faith that many students and critics alike tend to find baffling if not hollow—the hero's search for identity seems to have come to a dead end.

What makes teaching the central theme of *Invisible Man* more difficult still, and more interesting, is that Ellison himself posits a conception of identity that is quite different from that of his title character. Like many of us, the invisible man thinks of identity as something he achieves as the result of his efforts in a particular line of work or as something one has bestowed on him as a consequence of his meeting society's expectations for accomplishment more generally. In his view, it begins as a vague yearning for some "proper reflection of my importance" (160) and takes early form as a blueprint or life plan. In the end, however, it becomes something hard and permanent, a monument, even a fortress, against the ravages of time and chaos. By contrast, Ellison conceives of identity as something more basic to the self, something deeper yet more evanescent, something not static but dynamic and at the same time transcendental, in the sense that Ralph Waldo Emerson—the man for whom Ellison was named—thought of it in "Self-Reliance," his essay on the spirit that speaks within us all.

Ellison's conception of identity is presented only incidentally in the novel; like the invisible spirit that moves in everyone, it makes its appearance only at times of special vulnerability or openness. In several scenes spaced throughout the narrative, when the invisible man is on stage speaking or simply blurting out what is in his soul, typically using a jazzlike argot, he does in fact find himself, momentarily becoming truly visible to other characters in the book as an incarnation of what Ellison, using a metaphor from his apprenticeship as a trumpeter, called "the bungling bugler of words" (111). Beginning even with his obsequious address at the white men's smoker in chapter 1, the invisible man is always at his best, always his truest self, on those few occasions when he suddenly starts improvising before a crowd—asserting himself "within and against the group," as Ellison said the early jazz musicians did in defining their identities in every solo performance (*Shadow* 234). The invisible man achieves a sense of identity not permanently but intermittently, and not by conscious manipulation but, as Ellison himself does, by skillfully improvising his own version of what lies buried deep within us all.

In introducing the more conventional view of identity as the invisible man understands it, I find it useful to offer my students some background information on the subject generally, to speak (briefly) about the history of the concept and its significance as the crucial stage in a young person's development. I point out that—although thinking about the self goes back at least to Socrates—systematic study of identity is the product of modern psychology, beginning with the work of William James and Sigmund Freud at the turn of the century and culminating in the 1950s and 1960s in the psychosocial studies of Erik Erikson, particularly his *Identity: Youth and Crisis*, a condensed version of which appears in the *International Encyclopedia of the Social Sciences*. Of course, as students understand, people before the twentieth century had identities, too, but as a rule their identities were born into them as they necessarily followed in the footsteps of their parents in matters of work, religion, social class, and the other common determinants of identity. Away from the western frontiers of America, anyway, there was still relatively little social mobility such as one finds in the United States today and thus little personal mobility as well, little of the weighing of choices regarding vocation, domestic arrangements, and even class that young people in particular customarily face now.

Because the search for identity is a common theme in American letters, where stories of youth and outsiders constitute a major current, most students in a course on American literature are already familiar with the idea, at least as a general proposition, when they come upon *Invisible Man*. Moreover, because the effort to form an identity is the principal psychosocial activity of young people everywhere, according to Erikson, it is something about which undergraduates of all ages have some firsthand knowledge. Thus, in teaching *Invisible Man*, usually to students of varying abilities and levels of confidence, I begin by canvassing the class about their understanding of identity and of the sources of identity strength in their own lives. This exercise brings home to them, particularly to those who have enjoyed relatively privileged lives, the painful lessons of racial oppression and identity denial that are dramatized in Ellison's novel. Specifically, they come to understand that virtually everything they might name as a source of identity support (except the family, which Ellison, for reasons to be touched on later, necessarily plays down) is finally denied the invisible man: his name, his school and youthful achievements, his plans for the future, his past, even for a time his personality, and his freedom to think for himself in his own work. More important, as a man whose life is repeatedly dislocated, as he is forced to move from the South to the North through a series of picaresque episodes marked by dismissals, rejections, and violence, he lacks the feeling of coherence, what Erikson calls a "subjective sense of invigorating sameness and continuity" (*Identity* 19), that characterizes the healthy, independently functioning person. With increasing desperation, and yet with growing intuitive savvy, too, he is seen to hang onto the remnants of his past—the briefcase awarded him at the smoker, the link from the leg chain of Brother Tarp, the broken pieces of the bank he discovered at Mary Rambo's, the Sambo puppet left over from Tod Clifton's vending case—for these things constitute something of an identity for him, however tenuous and fragmented. Near the end of his search for his true self, after he has discovered Brother Jack's blindness to him, and begun to accept his past, he finally recognizes that all his past humiliations were more than separate experiences: "They were me," he says; "they defined me" (496).

After considering the subject in this personal, impressionistic way, we look more closely at the book, particularly at the way Ellison has structured his theme. *Invisible Man* falls into two distinct parts corresponding roughly to the title character's experience in the rural South and urban North, each part dramatizing a fundamentally different approach to the task of self-definition. In the first part, which extends well into the northern chapters while the hero continues to dream about returning to the southern black college that he has been forced to leave, the invisible man tries to form an identity by modeling himself after another man, his identity ideal, Dr. Bledsoe, the college's leader and latter-day incarnation of Booker T. Washington. In the second part, which begins in chapter 13 (the middle chapter of the book) when he comes under the eye of Brother Jack while giving an impromptu speech at a Harlem eviction site, the invisible man tries to "define" himself, as he says, by serving an organization, the powerful Brotherhood, Ellison's disguised version of the Communist party (428).

In examining Bledsoe as the invisible man's identity model in the early chapters, it is necessary to look both at Ellison's ironic treatment of his character and at the historical figure of Booker T. Washington, the influential leader and chief spokesperson of black people in America during the early modern era. We discuss what it is about Bledsoe—his power and prestige, his Cadillacs and creamy-complexioned wife—that makes him "the example," as the invisible man says, "of everything I hoped to be" (99). And then we discuss what the selection of Bledsoe as a model tells us about the invisible man and about Ellison's perception of the reigning values—white, middle-class, materialistic—in America more generally. It is necessary, too, to investigate the invisible man's reasons for persisting in his desire to be Bledsoe's assistant, even Bledsoe's "double," after the older man has sent him packing from the college, as well as his reasons, when young Emerson reveals to him the true contents of Bledsoe's damaging letters of recommendation, for becoming so enraged that he vows to return to the college and kill Bledsoe. Broadly speaking, his is the rage of many young men against the repressive power of the "father" and conversely against their own impotence and blindness. In the end, it is the rage of virtually every young man against his reluctance to grow up, to become—as the crazy war veteran advises the invisible man on the bus in New York—his own "father" (154).

Most college students are quick to perceive that Bledsoe is a treacherous role model having little more than his own interests at heart. As a rule, however, they do not recognize that the legendary figure of Booker T. Washington broods behind Bledsoe, both in the form of the nameless Founder, whose position at the black college and in the life of the nation at large Bledsoe has assumed, and in Bledsoe's own character as a deceptive, scheming black leader of immense national influence. To help my students to fill in the biographical background and to understand the larger social and political issues that center on Bledsoe's character, I ask them to read selections, if time permits, from Washington's *Up from Slavery* and at least chapter 3 of *The Souls of Black Folk*, W. E. B. Du Bois's historically important attack on Washington's policy of "accommodationism." It is this policy, in a slicker, more current form, that Bledsoe incarnates. If the course assignment schedule is cramped, I supply much of the background information myself in class, alternately lecturing and reading passages from the two supplementary works. But either way, I make sure students do not confuse Bledsoe, a caricature of Booker T. Washington, with the famous leader himself, a man of greater complexity and much greater good will. At the same time, I try to make clear that Ellison, siding with Du Bois in the debate over the nation's racial policy, strongly objected to the posture advocated by Washington (and still accepted in much of America when Ellison was writing his novel) when the black leader agreed to sacrifice what Ellison has Bledsoe call the personal "pride and dignity" (142) of his people, and their civil rights and political power as well, in exchange for concessions from white America for black people's vocational training and economic development. Ellison's position is perhaps most evident at the opening of chapter 1, in his ironic invocation of Washington's famous "Atlanta Compromise" speech of 1895, in which the black spokesman promised his white listeners that "[i]n all things that are purely social we can be as separate as the fingers, yet one as the hand in all things essential to mutual progress" (332). Yet Ellison's position is evident, too, in his ironic treatment of Bledsoe and in his linking of Bledsoe with the Founder in the memorial speech of the blind orator Homer Barbee, particularly in Barbee's blithe assurance to his young audience that Bledsoe possesses a "greatness worthy of your imitation" (131). It should be stressed, however, that Ellison is more concerned to condemn the practice of imitating Booker T. Washington or of holding him up as an example to others than he is to condemn the man or his policy. As the invisible man says in the introduction to his tale, life's hardest lesson for him has been the discovery that "I am nobody but myself"—that one cannot find oneself by accepting other people's answers to life's most fundamental question (15).

Who the invisible man is, following his disillusionment with Bledsoe, remains a mystery, even to himself, at least until the concluding pages of the book. But his desire to murder the deceitful black leader is at least a sign that there is something within him—a healthy kernel of pride, a vital ego struggling to assert itself—that is stronger than the fatal, narcissistic longing for adulation and the trappings of self-worth. In considering the middle section of the novel, therefore—chapters 10, 11, 12, and 13—I emphasize that the invisible man seems headed for a fresh, if not entirely promising, start in the development of a personal sense of identity. He still lacks a sense of life purpose, beyond his desire to earn the money to carry out his plan of revenge against Bledsoe. But in other respects he shows himself making appreciable gains, particularly in self-confidence and self-regard. The class and I examine the scene in which he stands up to the paranoid old boiler-room engineer, Brockway, and the later one in which he jokes sarcastically with the doctor in the hospital following the paint-factory explosion. Both scenes demonstrate that he has conquered his fear of people in positions of authority and at the same time found a source of authority within himself that he had never recognized before (221, 243). When he emerges from the hospital after reliving a version of his birth experience—a gruesome episode involving electroshock treatments that my students typically find both incredible and fascinating—he acknowledges, "I had been talking beyond myself, had used words and expressed attitudes not my own, . . . I was in the grip of some alien personality lodged deep within me" (243). We also talk about his eagerness to buy some hot buttered yams from a street vendor—one of several inconspicuous and unlikely wisdom figures in the book—which shows that he has suddenly come to accept his lowly southern past and, as a result, discovered a totally new sense of "freedom." "[T]o hell with being ashamed of what you liked," he thinks, savoring the yams' hot sweetness in the cold New York air. "No more of that for me." To the vendor, he exclaims, "I yam what I am!" (258–60).

Following a period of convalescence in Harlem at the home of a surrogate mother named Mary, the invisible man decides to take a job with the Brotherhood. Although he had initially dismissed Brother Jack's invitation to go to work speaking for the organization, now economic hardship is pressing on him, and he is beginning to feel like a free-loading child at Mary Rambo's. After I have briefly outlined the developments of this interlude, when the invisible man runs the risk of losing his newfound independence under Mary's smothering care, I invite discussion on the various ways the invisible man's emerging sense of identity is suddenly undermined by the Brotherhood, particularly its ruling elite. During the party scene when he is welcomed into the fold, one member whispers that he is not black enough for a future leader; another encourages him to think of himself as the new Booker T. Washington. Before long, he is even told to "put aside" his entire past and is given a "new identity," a new name (301–02). Though he confidently vows to himself, "[T]o hell with this Booker T. Washington business. I would do the work but I would be no one except myself—whoever I was" (303–04), it is clear from the start that he jumps from the frying pan into the fire when he leaves Mary's for a new life with the Brotherhood. The "self-mocking" image of the Negro coin bank that he finds just as he is leaving his room at Mary's serves as a symbol of his willingness, and need, to sell himself to make a living. For Ellison, who set his book vaguely in the thirties when the country's economy was in shambles and poverty was almost the norm, the struggle to realize the self never takes place in a vacuum but occurs in the context of powerful social and economic forces that always seem beyond the individual's control.

While most college students know something of the turbulent history of the depression, few of them, I have found, know much about the Communist party's sudden surge of popularity in America during that era. Thus it is hard for most of them to understand, in anything but a shadowy way, the social and economic issues and the racial and political conflicts that form the bases of events in the last half of *Invisible Man*. Even the Marxist undertones of key words like *science* and *history*, as used by members of the Brotherhood, remain something of a mystery to many of today's undergraduate readers. Yet outside a course focusing on the writings of the 1930s, those who teach the book will hardly have time to offer more than a few remarks about the growing involvement of America's underclass and middle class, of its writers and intellectuals, in the politics of the Communist party during the period. Teachers ought at least to survey the literary history for themselves, however, by reading Daniel Aaron's *Writers on the Left*, particularly parts 2 and 3, "The Appeal of Communism" and "Disenchantment and Withdrawal," a two-part pattern that parallels that in *Invisible Man*. Ellison himself has recorded only scattered remarks about his involvement with the political Left (although he wrote for the *New Masses* early in his career, with encouragement from Richard Wright, he was never connected with the Communist party). *Shadow and Act* (14–16 and 168–69) and Ellison's March 1967 interview (Cannon et al. 86 and 88) are especially useful here, as is Richard Wright's autobiographical essay in *The God That Failed*. In his essay, Wright provides a historically illuminating exemplum and enough parallels to the details in the narrative of *Invisible Man* to suggest that Ellison probably had Wright's experience in mind while composing the second half of his novel. Wright's essay is also short enough to be assigned to the class as supplementary reading.

    In tracing the course of the invisible man's involvement with the Brotherhood, I stress his growing self-deception—his eagerness, even desperation, to win from the world some acknowledgment of his existence, no matter how tenuous or false. I do so to emphasize what first-time readers of the book tend to overlook amid the more evident signs of his manipulation by the leaders of the organization, namely, that the invisible man is, to a significant degree, the master of his own destiny—the maker of himself (see 560). From the moment of his first talk with Brother Jack, he knows that the Brotherhood advocates the impersonal Marxist conception of history; he knows that, to the central committee, individuals—such as the old couple at the eviction site—"don't count" (284). Yet before long he permits himself to become so absorbed in the cause as to feel, as he says, "a wholeness about my work and direction such as I'd never known" (396). And in confrontations with the black nationalist leader of Harlem, Ras, and then with the narrator's new "double," Tod Clifton, after Clifton has dropped out of sight, the invisible man talks as though he has come to believe the Brotherhood's rhetoric concerning its ability to provide all that is needed for one's self-realization. Each time, he argues that only in "history" can black men such as themselves achieve visibility; only in the Brotherhood, he says, "could we make ourselves known" (424). Ironically, at the very moment the invisible man is congratulating himself on his unprecedented sense of accomplishment, the odious Brother Wrestrum—soon to charge him with the crime of being a "petty individualist" (392)—is mounting the attack on him that will lead to his falling-out with the Brotherhood. Even so, not until he is reprimanded by the organization's leadership much later for exercising "personal responsibility" in the planning of Clifton's funeral does he come to see that the Brotherhood offers no chance for him to think for himself or be himself. He realizes that, to the Brotherhood, the color of his skin makes no difference because the Brotherhood sees neither color nor men (497). What it sees, when it looks at him, is simply a faceless machine to be manipulated for its own ends, the twentieth-century equivalent of a slave.

Ironically, the narrator never seems to appreciate that there are occasions in his life when a mysterious "invisible man" such as we all have within us comes alive—occasions when his essential self becomes visible, if not to himself, then at least to others. In four major scenes—the men's smoker in the opening chapter, the Harlem eviction episode, the narrator's first Brotherhood rally, and the street funeral for Tod Clifton—the invisible man is shown on stage, momentarily finding himself while fumbling for words before a crowd, speaking out, if only at last, what is in his heart. I find it instructive to look briefly at all four scenes because together they show a progressive development in the narrator's inner self and a growing mastery of his jazzlike idiom.

The invisible man's first speech in the book, following the battle royal, is one he has given before and carefully memorized; it is full of big words and in other ways has been designed to impress the white establishment figures with his precocious ability to deliver what such people of the time typically wanted and expected to hear. Although he is awarded a leather briefcase and a college scholarship in the end, it is only when he departs from his meticulously prepared text, inexplicably blurting out the forbidden phrase *social equality*, in place of the smoothly worn, accommodationist term *social responsibility* (30–31), that his true self momentarily emerges. Only then, in turn, do the white clubmen, drunk and laughing with scorn, stop their revelry long enough to regard him as real; only then do they see him as something other than the stereotype of the humble, self-effacing black entertainer of old.

By contrast, his second speech, which occurs shortly after his accommodationist self has been destroyed in the paint-factory explosion, is almost purely spontaneous. Stumbling on a Harlem eviction, he suddenly discovers his capacity to identify with the suffering of displaced black people like himself. He also discovers the race consciousness that he had attempted to deny while at college, as evidenced in the Trueblood episode. Significantly, like the great performers of jazz music so important to Ellison, he struggles, at least in the initial stage of exhortation, both within and against the crowd. At first fearful of what the sight of the group's violence might release in himself, he suddenly starts to talk "rapidly without thought" but out of his "clashing emotions" (269). Like the trained jazz musicians, he does not give a perfectly spontaneous or abandoned performance, however, particularly after he begins to find his voice; as Brother Jack observes to him afterward, "Your emotions were touched" but they were also "skillfully controlled"

(283), a claim that gains credence when it is recognized that the invisible man had long studied and aspired to be a speaker (372).

The scene of his third speech, when the invisible man officially addresses a scheduled Brotherhood rally for the first time, shows him advancing to "a new phase," as he says vaguely, "a new beginning" (327). Again he finds himself initially at odds with his audience, wanting "to please" but at the same time feeling that he "did not trust" the crowd (330). Once he opens up enough to make "contact" with just one other person, however, it is as though he has been put in touch with "them all," and he is able, despite having forgotten "the correct words and phrases from the pamphlets" he had been studying, to begin to improvise on a theme of "tradition" (333). Then, in the midst of his presentation, he starts explicitly to testify to the miraculous change that at the very moment is taking place within him, the sudden feeling that he has "become *more human*," that with the eyes of the crowd on him he has at last "come home" (337–38). By the end of chapter 16, it is evident that he has been rapidly achieving, even while on stage, what Erik Erikson calls "the wider identity" (see the last chapter in *Identity*), the sense of being that accompanies identification with all the members of one's species, not just those of one's own race.

The funeral of Tod Clifton provides the occasion for the title character's final speech and the spur to the last stage of his development—beyond identification with race, beyond even identification with humanity or "brotherhood," beyond ideology altogether. Again, when he takes the stage, he speaks in an improvisatory way; and again he feels "a sense of failure" at his inability to "bring in the political issues" as the Brotherhood would have wanted him to do (448). But this time his speech transcends such concerns, aspiring instead to the level of music—as, indeed, it is inspired by music, by the mournful duet of the husky-voiced old baritone and the pure-toned euphonium horn that rose up spontaneously from the crowd and "touched upon something deeper than protest, or religion" (442) and stirred them all. When the invisible man has completed his friend's eulogy—a marvelous piece of vernacular poetry, Ellison's simplest yet possibly his most eloquent demonstration of skill as an "improvisatory" writer—he senses that, though the crowd is silent, it affirms his own identity, directing "many things . . . toward [him] through its eyes." When he takes one last look at the people silently waiting as the procession passes between them, he sees this time "not a crowd but the set faces of individual men and women" (448). An individual himself now, free of the Brotherhood's hold, he can see the people in this funeral-gathering to be individuals all.

As the book's several platform scenes suggest, Ellison regarded the making of one's true identity as an art of improvisation comparable to the performance of jazz. Ellison, who originally trained to be a musician, has written extensively on jazz music and its early legends. But "The Charlie Christian Story," an essay in *Shadow and Act* on the first master of amplified guitar, is especially pertinent to the study of *Invisible Man*'s theme, narrative structure, and technique. Because it stresses the strenuous social aspect of the process of identity formation, it serves also to explain the invisible man's vow in the epilogue that "the hibernation is over" (567). For it makes clear the need, if one is to forge an identity worth having, to come out of hiding and rejoin the human fray, as Ellison himself does every time he publishes a new work or makes a personal appearance. One passage in particular from the essay deserves to be quoted in full to the class:

> There is . . . a cruel contradiction implicit in the [jazz] art form itself. For true jazz is an art of individual assertion within and against the group. Each true jazz moment (as distinct from the uninspired commercial performance) springs from a contest in which each artist challenges all the rest; each solo flight, or improvisation, represents . . . a definition of his identity: as individual, as member of the collectivity and as a link in the chain of tradition. Thus, because jazz finds its very life in an endless improvisation upon traditional materials, the jazzman must lose his identity even as he finds it. . . .   (*Shadow* 234)

To illustrate to the class something of this fleeting quality of identity making—and of the remarkable persistence of the self, its resilience in spite of change—and to conclude our study of *Invisible Man*, I play several cuts from *Solo Flight: The Genius of Charlie Christian*. This two-disc album contains most of the recorded work of an extraordinarily inventive man, who died while still in his twenties, just months after he began to gain national prominence.

Invisible Man and the European Tradition

Leonard Deutsch

The widely variegated sources and richly allusive texture of Ellison's *Invisible Man* make teaching it both arduous and exhilarating. The encyclopedic range of Ellison's references to works in the European tradition adds provocative dimensions to the novel that most students will not recognize without guidance. Moreover, the length and complexity of the Western literary and intellectual works with which Ellison undergirds *Invisible Man* present special difficulties. For in his attempt to become a "Renaissance man," Ellison wanted to master all relevant cultural traditions: classical music as well as jazz, classical literature as well as the vernacular—in short, the best of whatever was available.

In *Shadow and Act*, Ellison provides some idea of the extent of his reading. Indeed, he claims to have "read everything" (16). He specifically refers to the European writers Auden, Balzac, Charlotte Brontë, Cervantes, Chekhov, Conrad, Defoe, Dickens, Dostoevsky, Eliot, Ford, Freud, Gide, Gogol, Hardy, Hegel, Homer, Joyce, Kafka, Kierkegaard, Malraux, Mann, Marx, de Maupassant, O'Casey, Racine, Lord Raglan, Sartre, Shakespeare, Shaw, Sophocles, Stendhal, Tolstoy, Villon, and Yeats—a bewildering and intimidating list for any freshman, to which critics have obligingly added more names, such as Vergil, Dante, Sterne, and Céline.

I believe that any meaningful and thorough analysis of *Invisible Man* requires the reader to confront the embryonic materials from which the novel was born. Ellison himself has considered the role of literary influences in his work. The act of writing, he says, has necessitated

> determining my true relationship to that body of American literature to which I was most attracted and through which, aided by what I could learn from the literatures of Europe, I would find my own voice, and to which I was challenged, by way of achieving myself, to make some small contribution, and to whose composite picture of reality I was obligated to offer some necessary modifications. (*Shadow* xix)

Ideally, all students should have read a list of prescribed books by the end of their freshman year. Presumably, however, most students do not have as extensive a background as we would like, and, presumably too, most of us do not have an entire semester to devote exclusively to *Invisible Man*. Given these constraints, I have had success with the following format. Early in the semester I set three dates: one by which students should have completed their first reading of the novel on their own and by which they should have made a preliminary library search of secondary sources; the second date, for class discussion of the book (at which time the narrative level of meaning is covered: action, character, point of view, the most obvious symbols, etc.); and third, the due date of the term paper by which time students will have given the novel a second reading. If students are asked to explore Ellison's relationship to other authors, I compile a selected list from the writers cited in *Shadow and Act* and *Going to the Territory*. Students can be assigned or allowed to choose one work or author from the list early in the semester. Since some may have to resort to interlibrary loan, they should undertake their preliminary investigation of secondary sources as soon as possible. I put *Shadow and Act, Going to the Territory*, and the major bibliographies on reserve and encourage my students to mine them. Beyond producing papers, some students may be asked to give brief reports summarizing their findings.

Although Ellison has made a distinction between his literary "relatives" whom he cannot choose (e.g., Wright) and his "ancestors" whom he deliberately seeks out and studies (e.g., Eliot, Malraux, Dostoevsky, and Faulkner), it is not necessary and may not be possible for the student to distinguish between writers who were seminal influences on Ellison and those who provide adventitious parallels or who are cursorily alluded to. What *is* important is that these links place Ellison within a broad and great literary tradition. These connections provide an enlarged context for evaluating the invisible man's motives and actions; they illuminate the character's illusions or, as the case may be, his insight into experience. Echoes of other literary works permit Ellison to be ironic, critical, playful, and parodical by turns. Moreover, by enmeshing his protagonist within a larger tradition, Ellison suggests that on the lower frequencies, the invisible man speaks for us. His alienation, for example, shared by Kafka's and Dostoevsky's characters, is not the exclusive property of the black race. His search for identity, to mention another example, is an archetypically American preoccupation. Most significant of all, perhaps, is the implicit notion that the Afro-American is the product of an extremely complicated cultural fusion.

A logical place to begin this study of sources is Homer's *Odyssey*. If enough students have already read this epic, the instructor can lead the discussion, providing a model for what students should be doing in their term papers. An identification of the allusion to the Sirens in the very first chapter—the blonde is likened to "a fair bird-girl girdled in veils calling to me from the angry surface of some gray and threatening sea" (19)—can initiate a discussion of how this and other Homeric (not to speak of Joycean) elements reinforce parallels with the original epic and in what sense the invisible man's quest can be considered an odyssey. The invisible man's odyssey is not to find a place (such as Ulysses's Ithaca) or to reestablish harmony at home but to discover a self that is, if not in harmony with the world, at least in equilibrium with itself. In the process of searching for himself, he encounters a Polyphemus figure when one-eyed Brother Jack stares at him with "Cyclopean irritation" (463) and expects black people to behave like sheep; a Proteus figure in Rinehart, the tricky shapeshifter; a Homeric blind creator of mythic tales in Reverend Barbee; and a Circe or two. He participates in various battles, and he makes a number of descents into the netherworld (the Brotherhood's headquarters, the "Chthonian," which translates from the Greek as "underground"). Students can also see that the archetypal motif of descent followed by renewal or rebirth recurs significantly throughout the novel. If time permits, the instructor might note the *Odyssey*'s presence in other ways: the invisible man is so entranced by the campus that, like Odysseus in the land of the Lotus Eaters, he is loath to leave it; the Scylla and Charybdis he must steer clear of are the union and Lucius Brockway, who, appropriately enough, dwells in a deep hole where cauldrons of bubbling paint are brewed; Elpenor finds his parallel in Tod Clifton, another young innocent who dies an untimely death; and the similarity between Antinoös, one of Penelope's suitors, who is shot through the throat by an arrow, and Ras, who is speared through his jaws, are also noteworthy.

Among ancient texts, the Bible is omnipresent in black literature. Biblical verses fuse most perceptibly with folk elements in the spirituals, and Ellison weaves refrains from black religious music into *Invisible Man*, but he also sprinkles other biblical allusions throughout the novel. In turn, the invisible man is identified with Adam, Jonah (156), Judas (170), and, ultimately, Christ. When he falls from grace and is expelled from the Edenic campus by the wrathful Bledsoe, the hero is forced to find and affirm the transcendent godlike power he contains within himself. The vet at the Golden Day mockingly proclaims, "A little child shall lead them" (93), and by the time Mary becomes his surrogate mother in Harlem, the invisible man does discover "I yam what I am" (259) when he glories in the vendor's yams. This epiphany of self-acceptance echoes God's response to Moses, "I am that I am" (Exod. 3.14), when the deity is asked to identify himself. Later, during the riot, the invisible man's passage over the Harlem streets where shattered glass "glittered . . . like the water of a flooded river" (543) suggests Christ's reputed ability to walk on water. In the epilogue, the invisible man characterizes his painful experiences as the "spear in the side" (562), while the prologue contains the resurrective image of the "Easter chick breaking from its shell" (6).

If students have not read the *Odyssey*, it is not likely they will have read the *Aeneid*, either. But possibly a student or two has been assigned Vergil's masterpiece in a Latin class. One such student might focus on book 6 to explore the Cumaean Sybil's relationship to her modern counterpart, Sybil, in *Invisible Man*. As with the oracular sibyls of old, the invisible man consults her, but instead of providing information she turns the tables and attempts to use him. Discussion of Aeneas might also inspire some remarks about the Dantesque elements in *Invisible Man*, for the narrator not only "entered the music" he plays in his underground hole "but descended, like Dante, into its depths" (9).

Most students have read Shakespeare's *Julius Caesar* and readily recognize that the invisible man's funeral oration for Tod Clifton is modeled after Antony's eulogy for the dead Caesar. Like Antony, the invisible man professes, more or less, that he has come to bury Clifton, not praise him. "What are you waiting for me to tell you?" the invisible man asks, "and when I tell you, what will you know that you didn't know already?" (444), echoing Antony's assertion, "I only speak right on; / I tell that which you yourselves do know" (3. 2. 226–27). Both orators use a standard device of oratory: the rhetorical refrain, Antony's phrase "and Brutus is an honorable man," has its parallel in the invisible man's repeated assertion, "his name was Clifton (and they shot him)." In addition, both speakers defend the murderers ironically and disingenuously. Antony says: "they that have done this deed are honorable . . . and will, no doubt, with reasons answer you" (3. 2. 215, 218). Ellison's narrator says, "The cop? What about him? He was a cop. A good citizen" (446). And both gradually shift to a more emotional appeal; Antony cries: "My heart is in the coffin there with Caesar" (3. 2. 110), which is perfectly paralleled by the invisible man's lament: "He's in the box and we're in there with him" (447).

Ellison also makes use of more recent Continental and English authors. Some authors are alluded to only in passing—as when Kierkegaard's famous formulation is converted into "all sickness is not unto death" (11) by the invisible man, who carries his sickness within himself until he can convert it into art. Other authors, although quoted only in passing, seem to play a more prominent role in the novel. For example, in ironically describing the campus as "the best of all possible worlds" (154), a phrase from Voltaire's *Candide*, Ellison suggests the relation between the two works: that they chart the journey from naïveté to the loss of innocence, concluding with a commitment in both to cultivate one's own garden.

Moralistic concerns attracted Ellison to a number of nineteenth-century writers—including Dostoevsky. An obvious analogue that exists between the Russian author's *Notes from Underground* and the frame of *Invisible Man* is that both memoirs are penned by narrators who have retreated underground. Although the tone of his narrator is more sardonically whimsical, "Dostoevsky poses questions about the nature of reality, the meaning of social responsibility, and the limits of human possibility, all of which are pursued with lively interest in *Invisible Man*," according to Robert Bone in *The Negro Novel in America* (202).

Ellison is also indebted to Dostoevsky's careful rendering of the social upheavals during the twilight of the czarist era and the "aggravations of sensibility" (16) that attended them. As Ellison explains to John Hersey, Dostoevsky made him "aware of what is possible in depicting a society in which class lines are either fluid or have broken down without the cultural style and values on either extreme of society being dissipated." In this same interview, Ellison also notes that he discovered in Dostoevsky's portrayal of the sociodynamic "the rich fictional possibilities to be achieved in juxtaposing the peasant's consciousness with that of the aristocrat and the aristocrat's with the peasant's. This insight," he says, "is useful when you are dealing with American society" and its peculiar racial divisions: "You get your moral perception of the contradictions of American class and personality from such literature" (Hersey 15).

There is also no question of Ellison's debt to André Malraux. "[T]wo days after arriving in New York," Ellison says, "I was to read Malraux's *Man's Fate* and *The Days of Wrath*, and after these how could I be impressed by Wright as an ideological novelist" (*Shadow* 118). Malraux, he feels, more effectively assimilates revolutionary content into aesthetic form. Ellison describes his debt to Malraux in the introduction to Hersey's collection of essays: "Malraux's concern with the individual caught up consciously in a historical situation, a revolutionary situation, provided insights which allowed me to understand certain possibilities in the fictional material around me" (14). Kyo, the main character of *Man's Fate*, is such an individual. "A half-breed, an outcast, despised by the white men and even more by the white women," he seeks dignity for himself and others (70). This quest leads him to experience the "solitude, the inescapable aloneness behind the living multitude" (59); in his solitude he even surrenders to self-questioning: "What am I?" But ultimately, like the invisible man, Kyo believes "ideas were not to be thought, but lived" (69).

In addition, Ellison—like Malraux—explores the betrayal of political movements and dramatizes an apocalyptic, surreal moment when madness and violence predominate. Against the backdrop of the modern world in a state of chaos, both writers also explore the conflict between destiny and free will, fate and individual volition. Both speculate about values in an absurd universe and about achieving meaning and dignity in life. But perhaps the most significant connection between Ellison and Malraux is their view that "the organized significance of art . . . alone enables man to conquer chaos and to master destiny" (*Shadow* 83).

Other French writers with whom Ellison appears to have a literary relationship include Sartre, Camus, and Céline. In addition, at least two other Continental thinkers indispensable to a study of *Invisible Man* are Marx and Freud. Students might be asked to read *The Communist Manifesto* and excerpts from *Das Kapital*. Reading proletarian propaganda from the 1930s will allow them to see that Ellison is parodying Marxist rhetoric and attacking the Marxist notion of a deterministic historical dialectic. Any standard analysis of Freudian dream symbolism will elucidate the double entendres of Trueblood's incestuous dream with its riotous tumult of doors, grandfather clocks, tunnels, and "some kinda crinkly stuff like steel wool" (58). Such an analysis might also help students understand the womb-tomb symbolism of the factory-hospital machine in chapter 11 (the tomb of his old self, the womb of his new self): the sterile and weightless medium enclosing the invisible man represents the amniotic sac (233); the severing of the cord attached to his stomach node suggests both his fear of castration and his symbolic rebirth as the "umbilical" cord is cut (238). Freud's concept of the id and the superego will shed some light on Supercargo's name and function. Students should also note that young Emerson owns a copy of Freud's *Totem and Taboo* (177).

Ellison directly quotes Joseph Conrad. For example, the invisible man thinks: "I've sometimes been overcome with a passion to return into that 'heart of darkness' across the Mason-Dixon line, but then I remind myself that the true darkness lies within my own mind" (566). Students might also want to consider Ellison's claim that he studied Conrad's prefaces to learn how to achieve certain effects.

Joycean references occur when the invisible man is "exiled" from the college. For example, Professor Woodridge says of Stephen Dedalus: "Stephen's problem, like ours, was not actually one of creating the uncreated conscience of his race, but of creating the uncreated *features of his face.* . . . The conscience of a race is the gift of its individuals who see, evaluate, record" (345–46). To this observation, the invisible man later assents, thinking, "To lose your direction is to lose your face" (564). The protagonist's burden and his mission is, of course, to become an individual who knows himself before he pretends to speak for anyone else. Moreover, like Stephen, the invisible man suffers from poor eyesight—for which he develops a compensating insight. This insight leads both characters to make an artistic commitment to clarify and communicate (i.e., "forge" the individual and national "conscience") through the written word. And Ellison has confirmed that *Invisible Man* is "the portrait of the artist as a rabble-rouser" (*Shadow* 179).

In establishing his relation to the literary traditions that provide the forms and create the contexts of his rich fictive world, Ellison has produced in *Invisible Man* more than a topical statement about race relations. Indeed, since the boundaries of Ellison's literary tradition are so broad, and since to remain ignorant of the European tradition is to diminish one's ability to respond to Ellison's novel, teachers—and students—have their work cut out for them.

Invisible Man and the Comic Tradition

James R. Andreas

The traditions of comedy and humor offer students open access to the complexities of Ralph Ellison's *Invisible Man*. Often ranked among the ten great novels of the twentieth century, *Invisible Man* might well emerge as the *commedia* of its age. The hero himself invites such a comparison when he tells us at the outset that he "descended, like Dante, into the depths" (9) of the coal bin and his own condition. Indeed, Ralph Ellison draws heavily on the resources of humor available to the black artist through the two great traditions of Afro-American culture: native African and American folk materials, and the Anglo-European conventions of carnivalesque and picaresque literature. The students I teach, about fifty percent black and fifty percent white, are fresh out of survey courses that cover European, English, and American literature, so many of the allusions to classical comic authors I cite in this essay are familiar to them.

Humor offers the black writer—and the teacher of his or her fiction—an aesthetic perspective through which to view the nightmare of Afro-American history truthfully but playfully. As Chaucer says, "A man may seye ful sooth [truth] in game and pley" (Prologue, Cook's Tale, line 4355). Within the context of "game and pley," the author is permitted to attack a culture that physically and psychologically enslaved a race of people. The attack, like the slanging contests of Greek Old Comedy or the reciprocated insults in the Afro-American custom of the "dozens," is delivered in sport, somewhere between what Chaucer calls "earnest and game." The great comic writers —Aristophanes, Shakespeare, Beckett—have all taken joyful advantage of such comic license to turn the world upside down and to view the history of its institutions from the perspective of its perpetual victims: women, children, racial and religious minorities, and other groups of socially "inferior" people.

The temporary impunity granted the comic artist to "seye ful sooth" may be traced back to social practices students may be studying in their anthropology and sociology courses. The ethnologist Gregory Bateson speaks of ritual practiced in the Adaman Islands. During tribal disputes, "peace is concluded after each side has been given ceremonial freedom to strike the other." The "battle"—and one thinks of the sequence of such mock battles in *Invisible Man*—becomes real only when the symbolic blows are "mistaken for 'real' blows of combat" (182). The hero begins with a real battle that breaks out over symbolic confusions, when he is attacked by the white man in the streets at the very outset of the novel. When the hero learns to follow the lead of the grandfather to "overcome 'em with yeses" and "undermine 'em with grins" (16), he fights symbolically to expose real historical wrongs. This is the paradoxical way of the comic hero.

After the open frontal attack on American racism practiced by writers such as Frederick Douglass, W. E. B. Du Bois, and Amiri Baraka, students seem to appreciate the comic indirection of Langston Hughes, Ralph Ellison, and Ernest Gaines. In addition, the hero himself, often perceived as an alter ego for Ellison, is drawn into the series of cruel pranks that plague all participants in the occasionally insidious games of modern culture. The joke is on him as well as his antagonists, both black and white. Like the archetypal trickster to whom he has frequently been compared, the hero is both naïf and confidence man, victim and aggressor, scapegoat and prankster. The invisible man is Hughes's Boyd and Simple fused perfectly into a single effective character: at once intellectual and pragmatic, deadly earnest and humorous. "He has successfully tricked others," Edith Kern observes, "but has also provided them with enjoyment. He has triumphed over them but has also been persecuted by them, and he finally goes away empty-handed" (119). Kern is speaking here of the trickster figure in myth and literature, but she might well be discussing Ellison's hero. Within the ultimately inclusive world of comedy, as René Girard remarks, the finger is pointed at everyone—antagonist, hero, and often the author of the comic fiction itself.

The hero's dream at the conclusion of the novel—a common practice in comedy, well represented in the utopian visions of *The Birds* and in Rabelais's description of the abbey at Thélème—brings together the dramatis personae for debate, if not reconciliation. The hero's reaction to his imaginary castration-blinding is the "laughter" of ignorance revealed: "I now see that which I couldn't see" (557). The hero triumphs through his failures. He loses each of the battles of the novel: against his provincial community, Norton's college, Emerson's paint company, and Brother Jack's pseudo-Brotherhood, but he wins the war. As in the long tradition of comic heroes paraded before us by Robert Torrance, the hero loses repeatedly in the short run, precisely so he can win the longer race. According to the logic of inversion that underlies the paradoxical visions of Pauline Christianity and Erasmian folly, he is first, because he has been last so long.

There are several significant Yankee precedents for such comic practices. Strange as it may seem, I have used the films of Charlie Chaplin, several of the shorts and almost all the full-length films, to teach students about Ellison's comic techniques. (For obvious reasons, I consider Chaplin a fully American artist.) In *City Lights, Modern Times, The Great Dictator*, and *Monsieur Verdoux*, Chaplin fuses social criticism and farce in ways that could not have been lost on Ellison, growing up as he did in the age of *Charlot*. Chaplin's Charlie is the little guy, more sinned against than sinning, but a worthy antagonist for the rich and their system against which he does battle in *The Kid* and *City Lights*. The latter film deals with the ambiguities of "blindness" and "insight" that so intrigued both Chaplin and Ellison. In

Modern Times the vagrant hero takes on the machine, short-circuits it, in fact, much like Ellison's hero blows up the paint factory without really trying. Charlie is also thrown in jail for inadvertently leading a mob down the street that turns out to be a demonstration of support for the "Reds." Similarly, the hero of *Invisible Man* becomes a political pawn of the Brotherhood simply because he expresses his sympathy for an old couple evicted from a Harlem tenement. In *The Great Dictator* Chaplin plays both villain and hero, both the dictator and his victim, much like the invisible man comes to recognize his complicity with Norton, Jack, and the other tyrants he faces off. He says as much to Norton at the end of the novel when he meets him in the subway: "But I'm your destiny, I made you. Why shouldn't I know you?" (565). Finally, the tramp become trickster emerges as a fully fledged confidence man, a veritable Rinehart, in *Monsieur Verdoux* and *The King in New York*. The tramp, now suave and elegant, sponges off the women who would ensnare him and takes calculated advantage of the system that would starve his children. The comic heroes of Chaplin and Ellison reach a common radical solution to their problems: a life underground and a decision to participate in the confidence games that inform American culture.

Ellison himself has taken note of the peculiarly Yankee nature of his hero in the cleverly titled essay "Change the Joke and Slip the Yoke" (*Shadow*). Students should be encouraged to read and report on such articles and on some of the many interviews Ellison has given. In this particular article, Ellison quips that the grandfather reminds him more of Ulysses in the cave of Polyphemus than of Brer Rabbit in the briar patch. He also denies that he had the "darky entertainer" in mind as a source for the hero. Blacks learned what they know of confidence games from traditional American sources. The role of the "smart man playing dumb" might be "more Yankee than anything else" (219), and Ellison cites several prominent examples accordingly: Benjamin Franklin posing as the "natural man" for the French, Hemingway passing as a sportsman for his readers, Faulkner playing farmer for the residents of Oxford, and Lincoln posing as the country lawyer for a nation of true believers. From the interviews, students also learn to appreciate Ellison's identification with Huck rather than Jim in the greatest comic novel of the nineteenth century. They discover that it is the younger Emerson who wants to play Huck to the hero's reluctant "nigger Jim."

Emerson, Ralph Waldo Ellison's namesake, offers a passage on the nature of the comic that comes very close to "accounting for" Ellison's comedic vision. I quote it here in full for its pedagogic value:

> There is no joke so true and deep in actual life as when some pure idealist goes up and down among the institutions of society, attended by a man who knows the world, and who, sympathizing with the

philosopher's scrutiny, sympathizes also with the confusion and indignation of the detected, skulking institutions. His perception of disparity, his eye wandering perpetually from the rule to the crooked,
lying, thieving fact, makes the eyes run over with laughter. ("Comic"
159–60)

The passage, which I use occasionally as a discussion topic on exams, suggests
Ellison's roots in the American transcendental movement. The hero is the
comic naïf, embodying in himself, and striving after, the ideal. Dante has
his Vergil, and the hero is on the road, so to speak, with a "man who knows
the world"—the grandfather, the vet, Rinehart. He is divided in his scrutiny
of the world between sympathy and indignation with its "skulking institutions." The disparity between this inner ideal and the hypocritical fact drives
him mad, like the "moon-mad" mockingbirds who flip their tails in the faces
of the founders of these institutions (132). (I encourage students to look into
the lore of the mockingbird, which has long been associated with comedy.)

   The reaction to this incongruity between the "rule" and the "thieving
fact," students should be reminded, is laughter, not despair. Such laughter,
Kierkegaard tells us, signals the last stage of existential awareness before
faith:

There are thus three spheres of existence: the aesthetic, the ethical,
the religious. Two boundary zones correspond to these three: *Irony*,
constituting the boundary between the aesthetic and the ethical;
humor, as the boundary that separates the ethical and the religious. (448)

The hero learns the lesson of the grandfather and Rinehart, which is, in
Emerson's words, "to maintain an honest or well-intended halfness; a non-
performance of what is pretended to be performed, at the same time that
one is giving loud pledges of performance" ("Comic" 160). Ellison's concept
of invisibility could not be more fully defined. And Emerson's thought might
be as well represented fictionally in *Invisible Man* as it was in Melville's
Confidence Man a century before.

   Almost every feature of the novel, then, can be attributed to one comic
tradition or another. Accordingly, I encourage students to do papers or
prepare oral reports on one or more of the following topic areas, which I
simply list here: (1) the treatment of sources, both serious and humorous,
particularly Richard Wright's story "The Man Who Lived Underground";
(2) the use of blues music as a thematic and structural source for the novel
(the blues are essentially a comic form, beginning, to use Dante's terms, in
adversity and ending in felicity); (3) Ellison's Menipean delivery, mingling

styles in a polyphonic, surrealistic fashion; (4) the novel's picaresque, episodic structure, maneuvering a hero from "blackness to light, . . . from ignorance to enlightenment" (Ellison, *Shadow* 193); (5) the chameleonic character of the novel's trickster hero and the inflexible antagonists he faces off; (6) the hilarious encounters with white women who take advantage of the hero as they contribute to his understanding of the world; (7) the use of colloquial "manners" and folk motif; (8) the local focus of the individual segments and the encyclopedic range of the world; (9) the slapstick effects of narrative acceleration and stylized violence; (10) the "improvised," spontaneous appeal of the narrative; (11) the paradoxical use of pun and other humorous verbal effects; (12) the novel's indubitably comic themes of rebellion and accommodation, death and rebirth, survival and triumph. The short papers and reports on these topics are useful, because they require students to consult the literary encyclopedias and dictionaries in the reference section of the library.

Of course, each of these topics represents a potential scholarly paper as well as a student exercise. *Invisible Man* is infinitely rich in a comic achievement that can only be measured against the grand traditions of world literature that inspired and nourished it.

Invisible Man in an
Ethnic Literature Course

Neil Nakadate

For a number of years I have been teaching *Invisible Man* in three quite different but fairly common types of undergraduate courses: an upper-level course in the American novel, an introductory course in American literature and cultures, and an upper-level multiethnic American literature course that emphasizes prose and prose fiction published since 1950. My teaching of *Invisible Man* in the last of these courses is the focus of this essay, but before I discuss my approach to Ellison's novel in a multiethnic context (Native American, Chicano, Japanese American, black), I should make some basic observations regarding this course as a type in comparison to the other two (which are, I suspect, typical in their own ways of the introductory-survey genre).

Put simply, while courses in the American novel and in American literature and culture might include healthy selections from women and ethnic writers (e.g., Plath, Olsen, Didion, Ellison, Silko, Morrison, Walker), they tend to reflect established assumptions regarding American literature and experience—beginning with the assumption that there is *an* American experience worth identifying and talking about. These assumptions underlie most such courses currently taught, are typically reflected in our course titles, and apparently derive from critical and pedagogical habit. By contrast, a course devoted exclusively to ethnic literature develops out of assumptions of its own, including some radically different assumptions about nationality, ethnicity, and aesthetics; it asks some combative questions regarding what is "American" and what is "literary." Put another way: in a traditional course *Invisible Man* exists in a context that includes such canonized works as Franklin's *Autobiography, Leaves of Grass,* and *The Great Gatsby*; in an ethnic literature course Ellison's book is part of a self-defining (and in its own way self-contained and exclusive) context of reading by other black writers and by writers of other ethnic backgrounds. In the former type of course ethnic writers are assumed to be a part of (absorbed into) American literature; in the latter, they are apart from it. And, presumably, the strategies for, and lessons learned from, teaching *Invisible Man* in an ethnic literature course are different from those in a more traditional one. I consider this bifurcation of premises and pedagogies to be problematical and try to counteract its negative effects by asking, What, after all, are the premises and patterns of "our" American experience? and by probing for some underlying constants. In the light of Ellison's novel, and especially the epilogue and its sense of the complex American fate, this question might become, How is the invisible man's experience not only black but also ethnic, and not only ethnic but American?

My approach is to set up the ethnic literature course by using two basic texts with which students are often familiar but typically have an imperfect understanding: *The Scarlet Letter* and *Adventures of Huckleberry Finn*. My purposes are (in order of increasing importance) to (re)acquaint students with these key works by "establishment" writers and to reveal these standard texts in a new light; to provide thematic introductions and comparative references (not necessarily norms) for the ethnic literature to follow; to provide contrasting references for subsequent reading; to use these canonized texts to introduce—apart from ethnic considerations per se—some key social, political, economic, and cultural concepts that will prove useful for the entire course. (Since the first work I teach after the books by Hawthorne and Twain is *Invisible Man*, Ellison's novel becomes a pivotal reading for the course and our introduction to ethnic literature in its own right.)

In turn, I devote one class each to descriptive commentary on seventeenth-century Salem and on Hannibal, Missouri, in the 1840s. I point out, for example, that bibliolatry was de rigueur in Puritan Massachusetts and that the term *church fathers* had current as well as historical standing. I point out that when Mark Twain was Huck's age, slavery was in fact legal in Missouri by virtue of political compromise. These introductions to recognizable yet unfamiliar and alien American cultures are not only necessary prefaces for discussion of the respective texts, they help define culture itself and clarify the role of cultural norms in determining a society's attitudes toward sex, race, and ethnicity and that society's relation to deviant, disaffected, or dispossessed individuals and groups. Specifically, of course, the crises of Hester Prynne and Huck Finn come about because they violate generally accepted standards of behavior as codified into law: one commits adultery and the other helps a slave escape. The effect of this violation of norms on each individual includes a kind of internal exile—Hester is ridiculed and ostracized (but not banished) and Huck finds his freedom and fate both wedded to a raft drifting not north to freedom but (ironically) into the deep South. Further, I explain that Hester is both patronized and persecuted because she is a woman and that Huck is abused because he is a child and patronized because he is a "poor white." That is, a paternalistic society treats them as it does because of what Hester and Huck are in its eyes (frail and weak-willed womanhood and youth, benighted candidates for social and spiritual redemption), and this is clearly a function of stereotypes, prejudices, and cultural habit. Hester and Huck are, in a revealing way, white "ethnics."

Furthermore, these quintessentially "American" books by Hawthorne and Twain illustrate nicely the ways any controlling culture (which does not, of course, have to be a majority) maintains its dominance over subordinate individuals and groups—by means of self-serving charity, token indulgences, promises of social acceptance and financial reward, the use of confinement and isolation, the exercise of rejection and ridicule, the creation of insecurity and mistrust, and the manipulation of guilt. It is, for example, a crippling and nearly disabling loneliness that initially pervades Hester's modest cottage and Huck's squalid cabin on the edges of civilization, and later this loneliness and the insecurity it breeds give rise to their belief that—despite impulses that seem to them and to us humanly, emotionally correct—it is they and not the "system" who have erred and are deserving of punishment.

In short, the novels by Hawthorne and Twain illustrate "before the fact" that the kind of American experience we think of as "ethnic" is not strictly a function of ethnicity but, rather, a function of ethnicity, race, and sex (interestingly, both Hester and the disguised Huck experience firsthand how society treats women differently from men) interacting with such cultural forces as politics, education, and religion.

Of course at some point in the discussion of Hawthorne and Twain it is also observed that there are finally some key differences between the major characters in the novels—that is, between Hester and Dimmesdale and Jim and Huck. Despite their shortcomings and differences from each other—but because they are white males—Dimmesdale and Huck can be part of the dominant culture. Dimmesdale is already a member of his community's elite, of course, and Huck is a member (albeit a sometimes perplexed one) of Tom Sawyer's gang, which is, after all, a juvenile reflection of the culture at large. In fact, Dimmesdale's sex and Huck's race enable them to get away with behavior that is forbidden their closest companions. But Hester, a woman, and Jim, a black man, will never qualify for such membership; they are categorically excluded, relegated to life as members of a different social, political, and economic class. Once this observation has been made we are ready to start in on *Invisible Man*.

I use the prologue and chapter 1 to introduce *Invisible Man* and to make a transition to our study of overtly ethnic literary texts. In particular, the prologue introduces some key terms and concepts for the course as a whole: the invisibility metaphor, as it applies to the ethnic's self-image as well as to ways of "seeing" by the controlling culture; the ethnic's insight-identity-responsibility imperative; the condition of internal exile so characteristic of ethnic protagonists, whether that exile is physical (withdrawal to the illuminated basement), psychological (the hibernating consciousness), or both; and the highly rhetorical cast of the ethnic's quest for identity and recognition, the interrogatory urgency of such questions as "What did I do to be so black and blue?" My goal is to help students identify these central notions and terms and to make clear that the invisible man tells us in the beginning where he has arrived because he wants us to learn by reading his story how and why he got there.

Chapter 1, the famous battle-royal chapter, is not only a brilliant opening for the novel as a whole but a classic paradigm of ethnic experience. Specifically, I focus on the youthful protagonist's naïveté, ambition, and belief in the prevailing system and the way the town fathers manipulate education, indulge in stereotypes of race and sex, and exploit subordinate classes for entertainment. The young invisible man, like Rocky and Tayo in Leslie Silko's *Ceremony*, gives himself over to the white man's educational system in the belief that this will help him gain recognition and acceptance, a chance to be known and heard: "I wanted to deliver my speech more than anything else in the world" (25). He does not see that as one of the talented few he will simply be a token black, toting a white man's briefcase and weighed down by relics. He does not see that education on the white man's terms is simply indoctrination for subordination—and a rejection of ethnic community and personal integrity. His sympathy for the naked blonde is not enough to make him see that they are both being exploited for entertainment by white males, and he is too shocked to understand that their toying with racial and sexual taboos is one of the more vicious methods of asserting and reinforcing their dominance over black men. All this is, of course, set against the enigmatic deathbed confession of the grandfather and the baffling nightmare message, "Keep this nigger-boy running"—corroboration from the past and premonition for the future appropriate enough for a person intent on denying his own identity.

In teaching subsequent chapters of the novel, I try to point out ways in which Ellison sustains the various themes introduced in chapter 1 and ask students to be particularly attentive to four themes pervasive in ethnic literature—the themes of shame and guilt, language and identity, stories and storytelling, and the dilemma of (re)entry. For much of his life in the novel, the invisible man obviously has an almost reflexive sense of embarrassment and shame (for liking yams, for being black, for not yet having his life figured out). He has a vague and nagging sense of guilt (for "failing" in some way, for not being able to go home, for not meeting others' expectations). In short, like many other ethnic protagonists—such as Abel in N. Scott Momaday's *House Made of Dawn* and the narrator of James Welch's *Winter in the Blood*—he lives a life that often seems an unrelieved apologia for being.

Of course a firmer grasp of language (including names and naming) in its relation to identity might enable the invisible man to quit apologizing, but for a long while he is too willing to use a vocabulary chosen by others ("responsibility" over "equality"), to preach a gospel written by others (first the Founder and Bledsoe, then the Brotherhood), and to accept their names for him. Like the often impassive and obscure Issei of Toshio Mori's short fiction, the inarticulate Abel in Momaday's novel, and Richard Rodriguez

in the autobiographical *Hunger of Memory*, the invisible man is a consciousness in need of a language for self-definition. Ironically enough, it is listening
to others' stories and coming to understand them that enables him to finally
comprehend his own. Not only his grandfather, but the vet, Brockway, and
Tarp offer tales that eventually help him decipher and articulate his life.
Like Antonio in Rudolfo Anaya's *Bless Me, Ultima*, the invisible man is
provided with wisdom and vision from the cultural past. Like Milkman Dead
in Toni Morrison's *Song of Solomon* and Tayo in *Ceremony*, who finally
listen to the stories in song that enable them to establish family and cultural
ties, he attends at last not to purveyors of "history" like Bledsoe and Brother
Jack but to timeless storytellers nurtured in the ethnic idiom.

Finally, I focus on the ending of the novel and on the invisible man's
promise to fulfill his responsibility on his own terms and to "re-enter" an
American society of which he was never effectively a part. Like Abel, Tayo,
many of the protagonists of Ernest Gaines's stories, and Ichiro Yamada in
John Okada's *No-No Boy*, the invisible man rejects isolation and exile for
community, even though he has not yet discovered the strategy that will
make this decision viable.

Ellison's epilogue, written well before *Brown v. Board of Education* and
the efflorescence of the civil rights movement, is prophetic. In his illuminated hole, the invisible man is developing strength and absorbing energy
—physical power and intellectual light—and is on the verge of a new identity. Like Huck Finn he has had enough of "sivilization" and its discontents,
but unlike Huck he has discovered in exile a viable alternative to "Tom-
foolery" and sterile compromise: personal and cultural truths that enable
him to believe that "[o]ur fate [as a nation] is to become one, and yet many"
(564), that may yet enable him to become part of a newer, larger whole.
Ellison's novel, with or without the help of Hawthorne or Twain, seems an
ideal starting point for a multiethnic literature course, especially one concerned with the deeper American patterns in the fabric of ethnic life.

TEACHING THE NOVEL THEMATICALLY

Understanding the Lower Frequencies: Names and the Novel

John Cooke

Readers of *Invisible Man* should not find it surprising that Ellison, as James Alan McPherson has reported, takes pride in calling himself a college drop-out. At best, Ellison finds formal schooling irrelevant. The decisive educational experience in his own three years at Tuskegee—his personal grappling with *The Waste Land*—occurred out of class. At worst, as the invisible man so painfully learns, formal education is stifling. Ellison goes so far as to claim that it was his "good luck" that Melville, Twain, and Hemingway, some of the novelists he came to value most, were not in the Tuskegee curriculum (*Shadow* 160).

In the same essay Ellison suggests that such novelists are now "doubtlessly overtaught": so much research has been done on them that teachers are particularly likely to disburden themselves of elaborate contexts and to analyze labyrinthine motifs, rather than encourage the personal exploration Ellison found engrossing in his study of Eliot. In contrast to this overteaching in the universities, Ellison affirms again and again in his essays what his narrator calls the "back of school" training of jazz sessions, barber shops, and rough country preaching in which the dais does not exist and masters and apprentices mingle. Taking my cue from Ellison, I want to look first at why we should be leery of overteaching *Invisible Man*. Then I turn to one approach to teaching the novel—the focus on the meaning hidden in names—that allows us to bring "back of school" into our classrooms.

It has been Ellison's fate to find his novel become one of those "doubtlessly overtaught" today. Indeed, the major problem posed to the teacher of *Invisible Man* is that it teaches so well. We teachers can trace the interlocking patterns of dreams, letters, speeches, power sources, and boxing matches. We can chart the invisible man's progress through his recurrent deaths and rebirths, trips between upper and lower worlds, and confrontation of his oedipal conflict. We can point out lots of gardens and apples, symbolic briefcase contents, and bullfight pictures. Or we can explain historical contexts from grandfather clauses to Garvey; literary references to *Huckleberry Finn*, *A Portrait of the Artist*, the Calamus poems, and *Julius Caesar*; and stylistic variations only adumbrated by Ellison's own division into the naturalistic, expressionistic, and realistic.

Discussion of these patterns and contexts works well in class, and they do count. But we teachers are led to hog the action not only because these patterns are initially not very accessible to first-time readers of the novel but for two other reasons. Too often we teach this long novel in parts, admonishing students about subtle allusions that are developed later. I find myself saying, "Watch for the reappearance of that bloody butterfly from the battle royal" or "Note that humming power station on campus."

This tendency to gloss the text is accentuated by the particular difficulty of the early chapters. The mythic-allusive aspects of the battle royal, Trueblood's story, the Golden Day, and Barbee's speech pose the most difficulty to readers new to the novel, and generally it takes a few class periods to get past the hospital scene to the Brotherhood where the forces keeping the invisible man running become clearer to him, and to readers. By this point we have doubtlessly established ourselves as initiators into mysteries our students are certain they could never solve on their own.

When I adopt this role, my students are impressed. (So, in fact, am I.) But there is a problem. My role is uncomfortably like those of the mentors the narrator spends the novel learning to escape. My motives may be better, but my advice has been more like a father's than a grandfather's. At worst, I fear I've become "a trustee of consciousness"; that as our discussions continue and tests and papers loom, my students will undermine me with yeses and grins. My fears are provoked, most generally, by the novel's consistent focus on the inefficacy of mentors of all shades—Bledsoe, Norton, young Emerson, Mary, Jack, and Ras. But the two teachers who figure briefly in the novel are most apposite. I may not be, like Hambro, sticking rigidly to "the tempo of the master plan" and trying to cultivate a "scientific objectivity" (493), but Woodridge's approach seems disconcertingly similar to mine. The invisible man does remember his giving good advice—to create the uncreated features of his own face—but he still recalls Woodridge "pacing as though he walked a high wire of meaning upon which no one of us would ever dare venture" (345). Woodridge's approach, in short, negates the very advice he gives. Like him, I've been dispensing high-wire wisdom; my students may apprehend the novel's basic theme, put most succinctly by the vet's advice "Be your own father" (154), but I haven't encouraged them to follow it as they encounter the novel.

A better teaching model is provided by the man on the way to discard the old plans. His elliptical questioning—"Is you got the dog?" (170)—reminds the invisible man of what he had earlier learned "back of school" and leads him to reconsider his path. I begin to fear that I, like the invisible man, have felt compelled to stick to the plan, my plan. I can hear the man with the plans admonishing me, "You kinda young, daddy-o" (172).

When I stick to my plan, moreover, I usually misrepresent the novel's world; I overvalue the formal structures (the plans) of the above-ground world, underestimate the less definable forces (the chaos of underground). The contrast of these two spheres is made most explicitly in the final Brotherhood meeting when the invisible man is chastized for his acting out of "personal responsibility" (452). Brother Jack's attitude here is simply a balder version of Woodridge's: "We're graduates and while you are a smart beginner you skipped several grades. But they were important grades, especially for gaining strategical knowledge" (459). The invisible man responds by affirming "the whole unrecorded history" of "gin mills and barber shops and juke joints and churches" (460). His affirmation grows from a series of such oppositions that began when he set the "logical appeals" of university church services with their "firm and formal design" against "the wild emotion of the crude preachers" outside the university (109). Only by looking less at formal designs and strategical knowledge, more at the less shaped, even wild aspects of the novel's world, do we come closer to the basic forces from which the novel grows, the chaos that the folk figures, for instance, return us to again and again. Theirs is the world of the "lower frequencies" (568) where questions elude easy answers: What is that freedom the old woman in the prologue loves so well? What did the grandfather's advice mean? Why did they pick Poor Robin clean? Would Louis have thrown old foul air out?

Such questions, like the troubling strings of unanswered questions in the epilogue, lead us to remember that in the novel, as the invisible man finally tells Norton, all roads lead not to Centre Street but to the Golden Day. They lead us to a different sphere where, as Ellison writes, it "is more meaningful to speak not of courses of study, of grades and degrees, but of apprenticeship, ordeals, initiation ceremonies, of rebirth" (*Shadow* 208). They lead us into areas where we should question our "courses of study," how we teach and overteach.

Ellison's emphasis on the chaos underlying the American experience, the criticism of mentors, and the foregrounded patterning that seduces us into analysis makes my insistence that we avoid overteaching more, I hope, than a late blast of foul air from the nondirective teaching world of the late sixties. For, as Ellison stated in his 1953 National Book Award address, *Invisible Man* is characterized by "its experimental attitude, and its attempt to return to the mood of personal moral responsibility" (*Shadow* 102). I suggest, then, that in dealing with the novel we begin by creating conditions that approximate its world: we should encourage students to fashion their own experimental attitudes, and we should give them the personal responsibility of forming their own moral responses.

The first, and essential, remedy to our overteaching is simply to allow students to read the entire novel; they might then write a brief response or submit questions. But since teachers, like invisible men, do have a responsible role to play, we might well direct our students' attention to names, through which first-time readers can begin to fashion their responses to the novel. The central role of naming in Ellison's world is clear, from his preoccupation with his namesake, Ralph Waldo Emerson, and his youthful nicknaming of his brother Huck Finn to his assertion that in the "arduous task" of becoming an American "the difficulty begins with the name" (*Shadow* 166). Readers will find that, as so often in the novel, the end is in the beginning, for claiming one's name is the result of renouncing those mentors. The invisible man equates these actions near the close by writing, "So after years of trying to adopt the opinions of others I finally rebelled. I am an *invisible* man" (560).

Certainly, naming is going to figure during any assessment of the novel, and if we choose to raise the issue before students come to the text, we aren't giving away much. The first sentence is the claiming of a name, the first recounted action is provoked when the invisible man is called "an insulting name" (4). Equally to the point, by suggesting that students consider how names are used, we give them a task they can perform, no matter how limited the literary or cultural contexts they bring to the novel. (Suggesting, by contrast, that they look for the oedipal theme isn't a direction they can follow without substantial assistance.) Many of the names require only some thought and an unabridged dictionary to begin giving students ideas. It also makes good sense to put on library reserve the relevant specialized dictionaries, such as the *Dictionary of American Slang* and *Dictionary of Afro-American Slang*. The possible pitfall of this approach is, of course, that students will force meanings or waste time over names that lead nowhere. But many of the names virtually call for attention (Trueblood, Bledsoe), are explained in the text (Westrum, restroom; Tobbit, two bits), or are highlighted by their profusion (the names given Norton at the Golden Day) or discussion (Optic White).

The basic intention is to suggest that students begin to understand the novel's world as the invisible man does—through learning the power of naming to foster or hinder self-definition. I define naming in the broadest sense, including not only the names of characters, places, and historical figures but also epithets, from "ginger-colored nigger" (21) to "nigger in the coal pile" (553), to cite the first and last of the dozens applied to the invisible man in the narrative. It is easy to move from the role of symbolic names and epithets to two finally more significant aspects: the few cases in the novel in which names indicate that characters have fashioned and claimed an identity and the use of names as an entry to such central concerns as folk culture, power, and the American experience. I don't raise these issues until after students have read the novel, although others might wish to do so. And other teachers will find that the names lead naturally to other aspects of the novel.

Students inevitably begin by looking for symbolic import in names. I'm not bothered at all when they find symbolic meanings that differ from the ones either I or other students find, for in a novel in which deception is the rule it is fitting that names should most often be ambiguous, at best ironically applicable. Names, like B. P. Rinehart, are full of possibilities. The variety of interpretations of his name—*rind* plus *heart; pure* (from the German) plus *heart*; even, to one interviewer, a reference to the guitarist Django Reinhardt—is simply the most obvious example of how often in the novel names call up the illusory and contradictory ground underlying the neat worlds of the planners. Sybil and the Brotherhood in the Chthonian retreat know nothing of underground mysteries; the constellation of names focusing on Brotherhood are misleading, as with Hambro (one who "hams," or acts like a brother), or ironic, as with Kimbro (only one letter away from falsely promising to be a brother twice over: *kin* plus *bro*); the Golden Day offers the golden age as apocalypse. From characters as important as the Founder (to initiate but also sink, as a ship) to those as minor as Primus Provo ("first provoked," a designation that applies to the invisible man in the eviction scene but never applies to Provo himself), names suggest meaning, but of a kind not easily ascertainable. Only rarely are complex fates unambiguously revealed by names: Tod Clifton (a man who dies by "plunging outside history," as from a cliff) or Mr. Broadnax in Trueblood's dream (a name suggesting that close relations with forbidden "broads" will lead to an assault with an ax).

The novel does not often support the deterministic view such prophetic names as Clifton and Broadnax imply. Names are a good guide to identity in *Invisible Man* only when they are the result of a conscious struggle for self-definition, what Ellison refers to as the "achieved identity" reflected in nicknames (*Shadow* 222). Most of these attempts to change from Saul to Paul, in the grandfather's formulation, fail. Young Emerson's claim, "I'm Huckleberry" (184), is hollow (the invisible man better deserves this appellation); when Ras changes from Exhorter to Destroyer, he becomes the unwitting tool of those with plans more comprehensive than his; and Brother Jack, whose foreign extraction implies an adopted name, becomes identified not with the proletariat as he intends but with monied interests (*jack* is slang for cash) or emasculation ("ball the jack" [563], as the invisible man observes near the close).

But a few characters do claim identities embodied in their names. All of them share similar histories: they have refused to become embittered by the gross mistreatment of the planners, and they foster regeneration in the invisible man, who eventually joins their number. The vet is a veteran of life's hardest knocks and a healer, a suitable doctor (a veterinarian) for the animalistic world Norton's visit to the Golden Day evokes. Brother Tarp has also earned his name, an anagram of *trap*, as the contrast of his shackle with Bledsoe's emphasizes, and he is alone, significantly, in bestowing the designation of brother only after it has been earned. Even the raggedy man with the plans convinces us that he deserves the folk names he claims: "I'maseventhsonofaseventhson. . . . My name it Peter Wheatstraw" (172–73).

The man with the plans suggests two of the broader patterns of the novel that names lead to. (Indeed, a good model for using names as a starting point for cultural inquiry is the essay "On Bird, Bird Watching and Jazz" [in *Shadow*], in which Ellison begins by searching in Roger Tory Peterson's *Field Guide to the Birds* for the origin of Charlie Parker's nickname.) One pattern is the thread of black folk wisdom of the plan man's versing here. The invisible man will call on this heritage to survive the hospital death and rebirth, and Jack the Bear is, of course, an identity he finally claims. But bears, dogs, rabbits, and other folk figures crop up elsewhere. It was a student who first pointed out to me, for example, that the middle name of the seemingly servile Bledsoe ("Poor me, ain't I bled so") is Hebert ("a bear"). Consideration of such names leads directly to the black folk culture that is often passed over in a mumbling parenthesis. Names take us beyond such details as the echoes of the Atlanta Exposition Speech to the masking and signifying world of Trueblood, plan and yam men, Dupre's rioters, and others outside the world of the planners.

The queries of the man with the plans about whether the invisible man's got the bear or the bear's got him raise the central issue of power, also developed through the use of names. As the designations given Norton by those at the Golden Day indicate so clearly, the novel's world is one where conferring power or demanding subservience begins with names. To the inmates, Norton is first General Pershing (71), John D. Rockefeller, and the Messiah; but as his status declines, he becomes Mister Eddy (77), "a trustee of consciousness" (88), an "ole baby," and finally one of those white men "with monkey glands and billy goat balls" (86).

More centrally, the invisible man's growth proceeds through his learning to perceive the importance of names and finally to confer them. Initially seeing himself as "a potential Booker T. Washington" (18), he strives to be worthy of identities that suit the planners, and for most of the novel he is rendered powerless through accepting a variety of names—by the Brotherhood and those who see him trying to drop the Sambo bank, for instance. He makes his first small step in conferring his own names when he berates Brockway for being a "handkerchief headed bastard" (222), but he is still using the culture's ready-made slogans, which don't help much. Only near the close when the invisible man searches for meaning in individual names does he begin to define the world in his terms. The change is most evident in his eulogy built on "His name was Clifton" (444–48), but his references to Tobbit/two-bit, Westrum/restroom (504), and Tod/Tod (431) are also part of this process, not the gratuitous punning they have sometimes been called. Finally, he searches for his own names, first by trying out, but quickly rejecting, "Santa Claus" (a father figure, however benign) with Sybil (511). As the prologue reveals, he's still experimenting, having claimed not only "invisible man" but "Jack-the-Bear" (6) and "thinker-tinker" (7) for himself.

I hope that students will finally move to the more abstract process of naming foregrounded in the prologue and epilogue, where Ellison's protagonist realizes that finding his name is bound up with naming the abstractions on which his American experience rests. He provides his own definitions of "contradiction," "responsibility," and his current response of "hibernation." He struggles during his reefer-induced dream on the lower frequencies with "freedom." The definitions he provides are unorthodox, his own. I have suggested that we allow students to follow his example, to begin searching for the possibilities in the novel's world through Ellison's use of names.

The invisible man's closing words are an injunction to exercise such personal responsibility. He questions, "And this is what frightens me: Who knows but that, on the lower frequencies, I speak for you?" He is frightened, of course, because he suspects his condition is general. But does he not also fear that, like those mentors he has recently escaped, he has the urge to suggest who his listeners are? Our teaching of *Invisible Man* will be fully successful, I think, only when our students respond to his question, "I see. But I'll speak for myself."

Focusing on the Prologue and the Epilogue

David L. Vanderwerken

Some works are almost too rich, too teachable. *Invisible Man* is one such, a novel so *written* that an entire semester could easily be devoted to it. Few of us, of course, have this luxury. Thus, in my sophomore-level class, I adopt a thematic approach, focusing in particular on the prologue and the epilogue.

I have offered this particular course, The American Dream, for sixteen years. Designed for a general audience, it is more an ideas course than a literature class. It is really a course in American mythology. One aspect emphasized is the mythology of success, the process of self-making as it comes to us from the Puritans, Benjamin Franklin, and Horatio Alger, and the assumption that the universe itself will cooperate with the self-makers as they go about their self-making. The more complex attitudes toward self-making, those that ponder its implications for the individual and society, emerge in Hawthorne's *Blithedale Romance*, Howells's *Rise of Silas Lapham*, Fitzgerald's *Great Gatsby*, Steinbeck's *Of Mice and Men*, Miller's *Death of a Salesman*, and *Invisible Man*. All these works respond to Mr. Alger, "There are more things in heaven and earth, Horatio, than are dreamt of in your philosophy," with Ellison's novel providing the most complex response of all.

For many students, *Invisible Man* is the most difficult book they'll ever read, so it is crucial that they get a grasp of the prologue, where Ellison introduces the imagery, the styles, and several of the characters and distributes the themes he will develop for the next five hundred pages.

Much of the unity and continuity of the novel depends on Ellison's imagery of vision: seeing and blindness and all gradations between, foresight, hindsight, insight, the relations between sight and awareness, understanding and interpretation, and, of course, visibility and invisibility. Therefore, students must make sense of the definition of invisibility and the illustration Ellison establishes on the opening page of the prologue. The key phrase is "inner eyes" (3), by which Ellison means that what people see is a function of their picture of reality. Everything seen is a projection of the inner eyes, and that which the inner eyes refuse to see is indeed invisible. Ellison illustrates the concept in the prologue's first scene. The man whom the invisible man bumps into, who curses him and who won't apologize, had seen the invisible man not as a human being, a person, but as a phantom in his own mind. This vignette of seeing the preconceived and of refusing to see what the inner eyes' picture of reality cannot accommodate will be repeated dozens of times in the narrative.

Closely related to vision imagery and also introduced in that opening scene is a cluster of images concerning sleeping, dreaming, sleepwalking, and awakening, being in a state of awareness. The invisible man has learned that most people are "zombie[s]" (92) who sleepwalk and dream their way through life, never awakening to reality, like the man on the street whom the narrator characterizes as "lost in a dream world" (14) that nearly kills him. Students need to grasp this pattern of imagery because every time the invisible man grows more conscious of reality in the narrative, he speaks in terms of waking up.

A final set of images that students need to be aware of are those of black and white, darkness and light, and, again, the gradations between. The invisible man has wired his hole with 1,369 light bulbs. Before, he says, "I lived in the darkness into which I was chased, but now I see. I've illuminated the blackness of my invisibility—and vice versa" (13). Now, he is engaged in writing his autobiography, "to put invisibility down in black and white" (13–14). The novel inverts the traditional associations so that blackness and darkness illuminate while whiteness and light can blind, an inversion consistent in the narrative chapters.

The paradox of black and white parallels other paradoxes in the prologue that will be developed at length in the narrative. The narrator has learned that the nature of reality is contradictory and circular instead of rational and linear, that life is fluid, not fixed, that flexibility is necessary for survival. Many students have trouble with the prologue precisely because Ellison is trying to break down our picture of reality, our preconceptions about life, to prepare us for the complex vision of reality that the novel develops. Most of us want the world to make sense, and when it doesn't, we'll force it to make sense. Our hero has learned to accept, even to become comfortable with, confusion, has gained a maturity and wisdom in becoming "acquainted with ambivalence" (10). Ellison's prologue plunges us into confusion—which no one likes, students least of all—in an attempt to alter the way we look at life. Style itself is one way he achieves this effect. For example, the hallucinatory sequence in the prologue prepares us for the surreal style of many of the chapters. Hallucinations and dreams are frightening because in them the world is no longer nailed down. Students, like the invisible man himself, will overcome their fear of a fluid reality in discovering that infinite possibility is the happy result. This is no easy notion, but by the end of the novel, students usually get it.

Several of the characters mentioned in the prologue dramatize the idea that each person's living defines his or her picture of reality. The three mentioned—Ras, Rinehart, and Brother Jack—believe that the world is controllable. Such a notion has been "boomeranged" (6) out of the invisible man's head, and he sees that all plans and visions are tentative, revisable, and most important, relative.

The novel details the boomeranging process, and the epilogue summarizes the invisible man's learning experiences and underscores their significance for him and for us. Sometimes, however, my students overlook the expressly didactic task of *Invisible Man*: "What else but try to tell you what was really happening when your eyes were looking through?" (568). Like the ending of *The Great Gatsby*, the epilogue is expansive, reaching out to include us all today, to express our fear that we are part of somebody else's movie instead of directing our own.

I treat the epilogue as Ellison's reaffirmation of Emersonian self-reliance. The very sentences of the epilogue echo the famous essay. For example, "Whence all this passion toward conformity anyway?—diversity is the word" (563) and "Life is to be lived, not controlled" (564) could have been written as easily by Ralph Waldo Emerson as by Ralph Waldo Ellison. The epilogue celebrates diversity, tolerance, spontaneity, and community, while condemning manipulation, conformity, homogenization, and coercion. Students see that the invisible man only began legitimate self-making after he fell into the hole. Before, others were making him—Bledsoe, Norton, the Brotherhood—as he tried first to be an Alger hero, a black variant thereof, then a hero of collectivist politics. Now, disabused of models, he is puzzling out who he is and what he is to do by himself. As Emerson said in "Self-Reliance," "Nothing is at last sacred but the integrity of your own mind" (30).

The issues in the epilogue usually generate lively discussion since questions of identity and vocation are the deepest concerns of students, and they are willing to listen to the views of the invisible man, who is, after all, their age. The discussion can be painful, too: the question whether students are in school because *they* want to be there may open many wounds. The following discussion questions center on selfhood and have worked well in my class discussions of the epilogue:

Is selfhood defined in a vacuum or only in relation to others?
Is the self a resource adequate enough to answer all the self's questions?
Is the self a reliable arbiter for everything?
Is accepting yourself the truest form of self-making?
How does one walk the tightrope between what the self desires and what society demands?
Where does self-reliance shade into self-indulgence and narcissism?
Is it possible to live without being a puppet or a puppeteer?

Not only does the epilogue try to resolve the meaning of individual selfhood, but it also tries to resolve the problem of the individual's relation to America. This latter effort forms the second emphasis in my strategy for teaching the epilogue. Still "plagued by his [grandfather's] deathbed advice" to "overcome 'em with yeses, undermine 'em with grins" (16), the invisible man offers a series of possible interpretations, all having to do with affirming the "principle on which the country was built" (561), a marvel of intentional vagueness like Jefferson's "pursuit of happiness." I suggest to students that perhaps Ellison's phrase refers specifically to the self-evident truth that "all men are created equal," as well as more generally to the nexus of ideas associated with the promise of America. The list is usually sticky going for students. What I stress is the invisible man's celebration of the ideal, the "principle," as being larger than any person or group and inclusive of every person and group. I find it useful to refer back to chapter 25 where the invisible man, just before he spears Ras, thinks of all those reality directors—"trustees of consciousness" (88), as the vet at the Golden Day calls them—who refuse to "recognize the beautiful absurdity of their American identity and mine" (546). For Ellison, the health, strength, and beauty of American life lies in its heterogeneity: "America is woven of many strands; I would recognize them and let it so remain" (564). When students get bogged down in the eloquence, I use an unabashedly homely gimmick, pulling a coin out of my pocket and reading *e pluribus unum*. This is really what Ellison is reminding us of, "Our fate is to become one, and yet many" (564). Identifying and accepting ourselves is a patriotic activity; it affirms the principle. And, correspondingly, resisting those who would make us "conform to a pattern" (563) demonstrates fidelity to the principle. I think Ellison had to restrain himself from simply quoting "Whoso would be a man must be a nonconformist" (29). He does everything but.

In wrapping up the epilogue, I ask my students to think about our previous works in the light of the message on the next to last page: "And the mind that has conceived a plan of living must never lose sight of the chaos against which that pattern was conceived." We recall Crèvecoeur, who tells us in "What Is an American?" that an immigrant becomes an American when "he forms schemes and embarks in designs he never would have thought of in his own country" (McMichael 400). We recall Franklin, who "conceived the bold and arduous project of arriving at moral perfection" (103), complete with a scorecard and a timetable. We recall Alger's Ragged Dick climbing the ladder to bourgeois heaven—respectability. And we recall those characters who "paid a high price for living too long with a single dream" (*Great Gatsby* 162): Fitzgerald's Gatsby, Miller's Willy Loman, Steinbeck's George and Lennie, and Hawthorne's Hollingsworth—characters whose plans blew up in their faces. All these examples illustrate American innocence, a naive faith that not only can the self be remade by sheer will but that external circumstances can also be controlled. Our writers suggest that American innocence is very dangerous to the health since the body count in American fiction is rather high. Our hero, the invisible man, ends up alive and aware, although he has been whipped hard. He has learned that flexibility is the key to both survival and maturity. This wisdom is learned the hard way, through experience, although several truth tellers along his journey try to enlighten him. In chapter 9, Peter Wheatstraw, pushing his cart of discarded blueprints, tells the invisible man, "Folks is always making plans and changing 'em." Our nineteen-year-old says, "[T]hat's a mistake. You have to stick to the plan." While Peter Wheatstraw may not have read Fitzgerald, Miller, or Steinbeck, his response to our hero echoes their judgments: "You kinda young, daddy-o" (172). The invisible man may end up in a hole, but he has been cured of his tunnel vision.

Teaching the prologue and epilogue is an admittedly selective approach to teaching *Invisible Man*, a novel that draws together just about every topic in my course. Despite my narrow focus, "Who knows but that, on the lower frequencies, I speak for you?" (568).

"Ball the jack": Surreality, Sexuality, and the Role of Women in *Invisible Man*

Mary Rohrberger

Take an image. Assign to it significations that reverberate through a patterned narrative line; allow it to bounce back and forth as though between reflecting mirrors multiplying times, places, and situations so that beginning and ending can no longer be defined. Send the image spinning magically through at least three dimensions to collide with other images that are in some mysterious way variations of itself, so that all finally merge and are identified in surreal perspective, and you have a work of art hard to deal with in any linear, expository way that is ultimately the way of critical analysis and of much teaching. What critic or teacher is ever satisfied with analysis or doesn't know that a poem doesn't mean but is? What critic or teacher is ever satisfied with the simple tautology: a = a? So a rose is a rose; still we need to find ways to talk about it. And so yes does and does not equal no; still we need to try to explain the surrealist paradox.

Ellison knows what he is doing. He knows that only in art can the paradox be captured from deeper levels of consciousness where, as he says in *Shadow and Act*, "reason and madness mingle with hope and memory and endlessly give birth to nightmare and to dream" (100). The essence of the word, he observes, is its ambivalence, and "it is never so effective and revealing as when both potentials are operating simultaneously, as when it mirrors both good and bad, as when it blows both hot and cold in the same breath" (25). Ellison also knows that, as conscious of craft as an artist needs to be, still the subconscious mind puts all manner of things into juxtaposition, converting incidents into patterns, which when brought to the surface can be recognized as significant rituals of situation and can be raised to the level of art. It is a mistake to ignore the art, the craft, in the erroneous notion that one misses meaning by focusing on form. In fact, there can be no meaning without form, and when meaning is focused on paradox, what better form than surrealism, where the use of dream logic makes it possible for beginning to be end, up to be down, hope to be despair; where one can discover the silence of sound, overcome an enemy "with yeses and undermine 'em with grins" (16), and see around corners in a world that moves "by contradiction" (6)? In fact, what better mode than surreality to make concrete and visible a protagonist whose own inability to function is due to his invisibility and his powerlessness to deal with the nether world of ambiguity, myth, and universal guilt?

But a complex work of art like *Invisible Man* will not yield itself readily to analysis, because the more one sees, the more there is opened up to see, and a teacher must make choices. Surely, students should be helped to uncover some of the major patterns. Ellison himself has pointed out many of them: the pattern of constraint and constriction played out on historical, social, and philosophical grounds; the mythic quest for identity involving rhythms of death and rebirth; the uses of folk materials including the blues and the sermon tradition as backdrop and accompaniment; the design of the picaresque; the network of metaphors such as visibility and invisibility, illusion and reality, nightmare and daydream, surrogate fathers, and symbolic naming, as well as the many other approaches suggested by articles in the present volume and by books and articles published elsewhere. Teachers can choose what shall be emphasized by the types of questions they ask within the constraints of the course, the levels of student understanding, and the backgrounds the students bring. But certainly, whatever the immediate reason for discussing *Invisible Man* with students, in today's world surrealism as a mode of expression and sex roles are going to come up within the context of the whole.

Invisible Man is surreal throughout, not simply in the technique used in the latter third of the novel. Surrealism is not just a synonym for dreamlike. Rather it is a means of meshing affective and cognitive realms, of yoking together the apparently dissimilar in startling and revelatory ways, of allowing the subconscious to surface and combine with the conscious, of creating images so rich that they bounce crazily back and forth and up and down, gathering to themselves other images through a dizzying accretion until montages are built that carry implications far beyond any single act of signification.

I want to explore the image "ball the jack" to demonstrate how it functions in the novel to reveal an important aspect of theme by means of the surreal perspective. Sexual identity and sex roles are, of course, a part of the novel's major theme, but, surprisingly, very few critics have addressed the subject, and when they have, they focus almost exclusively on the Trueblood incident in an effort to show Trueblood as a potent folk hero having mythlike proportions, in contradistinction to the false fathers who populate the book. Trueblood refuses to castrate himself or to allow himself to be killed because of his "dream-sin"; and his anguish and pain together with his love of life ultimately are expressed in his blues songs. He knows what he did to be, in the words of the Louis Armstrong song, "so black and blue." The narrator of *Invisible Man* tells his story to explain why he is "so black and blue," and at the end of the narrative proper, before the epilogue, he recounts a dream where the fathers castrate him, taking a knife and holding him down until he feels the "bright red pain" and sees the "two bloody blobs" that they throw up over a bridge. But the bags of flesh catch on the curving arch of the bridge and hang there, "dripping down through the sunlight into the dark red water" (557). This dream castration is the climax of the novel. Since they couldn't keep him running, the fathers have dealt him the penultimate punishment for daring to rebel. In the epilogue the invisible man makes the point:

> Hence again I have stayed in my hole, because up above there's an increasing passion to make men conform to a pattern. Just as in my nightmare, Jack and the boys are waiting with their knives, looking for the slightest excuse to . . . well, to "ball the jack," and I do not refer to the old dance step, although what they're doing is making the old eagle rock dangerously. (563)

"To ball the jack." In his hibernation the invisible man calls himself Jack the Bear, and in this sentence he is clearly talking about himself; but the phraseology of the whole sentence suggests several possibilities that rebound through the novel like balls manipulated by a juggler and bouncing through every important sequence.

The battle royal is set up expressly by the white fathers to keep the black boys in their proper place. At the front of the room, the center of attention of all the drunken white men is a blond woman stark naked. Her face is heavily powdered and rouged. Her eyes are hollow and smeared blue, the color of a baboon's butt. She has an American flag tattooed on her belly. The white men sway to the music in time with the blond's dancing and moving hips. The narrator responds in a sexual way to the woman and to the situation, and he hates the woman for it. Simultaneously he wants to caress and to destroy her. Other young black boys are dissolved into jelly. One tries to hide an erection with his boxing gloves. In time, the drunken men begin to chase the woman, and when they catch her, they pass her over their heads, tossing her about while her breasts flatten out and her legs fling wildly about. In her eyes the narrator sees both terror and disgust.

Clearly the white men know what they are doing. They call the black boys to the front, at different times addressing them as "shines," "coons," and "Sambos." The white men openly exhibit to the black boys not only the white woman but their own sexual powers and then by means of the fight to follow cause the boys to punish themselves blindly and brutally for daring to look. In a sense, the battle royal is a choreography of masochism designed to accomplish the sexual satisfaction of the white male majority in a patriarchal society. But an even more effective means of making the point of the majority is the use of the electrified rug where the wet boys writhe in painful contortions. The narrator watches one boy "literally dance upon his back, his elbows beating a frenzied tattoo upon the floor, his muscles twitching . . ." (27).

The next important episode in the novel begins at the state college and ends when the narrator is cast out. Roles become more complex in this episode as black fathers are introduced and turn out to be mirrored reflections of the white fathers. The bronze statue of the college Founder and the slave stands as objective correlative of the role played by the black fathers. The Founder seems at once to be lifting a veil from the slave and fitting it more firmly in place. Barbee eulogizes the Founder, giving his life mythological significance and him godlike stature. According to Barbee, the Founder's death was followed by resurrection implicit not only in the fruit put forth every year by the college but also in the flesh of Bledsoe. Bledsoe lives for and through the power he has in his manipulative role. The shell-shocked veterans controlled by the monstrous Supercargo are led to the Golden Day for their day with the prostitutes. The veterans are a microcosm of a whole social order of black sons. They have been doctors, lawyers, civil-service workers, artists, politicians (one is even a psychiatrist). In the war they have seen a vision of a different society and a different role. Now they need to be controlled lest they rebel. As inverse images of the fathers who lie, the vets speak truth in metaphoric ways. They refer to Norton as grandfather, John D. Rockefeller, and the Messiah. Norton is one of the great white fathers, a friend of the Founder, who sees the college as "dream become reality" (38). Norton and Trueblood are also presented as mirror images of each other. Norton's interest in Trueblood's story is characterized by an urgency explainable only by the assumption that he must have shared a powerful attraction to his own daughter, now dead. And though Trueblood lives in blackness, Norton is an image of "a formless white death . . . a death which had been there all the time and which had now revealed itself in the madness of the Golden Day" (84–85).

Like Trueblood's sexuality, Norton's is mythologized. One of the prostitutes says that Norton is like other "rich ole white men," who have "monkey glands and billy goat balls" (86). The most articulate of the veterans tells the narrator that he is learning not only all about endocrinology but also about how myths are started: "he [Norton] was only a man; it seems now that he's either part goat or part ape. Maybe he's both" (87). While Trueblood is punished for his sin by his wife, who wounds him with an ax, Norton's punishment is more oblique, although sufficiently wounding to send him into a comatose faint. Norton, like Trueblood, comes to know what he did to "be so black and blue," but his knowledge is buried within himself and he will not allow it to surface.

Two scenes in this episode seem reflections of the dance that takes place on the electrified rug in the battle royal—the veterans' attack on Supercargo and the service in the college chapel. The attack on Supercargo is an attack by men restrained like children on a master who does the bidding of white men. Barbee's sermon is also dance. As he speaks he presses his fingertips together and with his feet together begins a slow, rhythmic rocking, tilting backward and forward on his toes until it seems that he will fall. As he talks, a rhythm is established, and oration becomes solo instrument played to the accompaniment of the emotions of the audience.

For acting on his own responsibility, the narrator is banished from the kingdom; and for speaking the truth, the veteran-physician is transferred. Both removals are metaphoric forms of castration. From both situations the narrator departs having learned nothing, even though the veteran-physician speaks plainly, telling the boy that he needs to learn to look beneath the surface, to come out of his fog, to play the game but not believe it. The most significant piece of advice the veteran gives to the boy is "Be your own father, young man. And remember, the world is possibility if only you'll discover it" (154). Believing too strongly in the American dream, the invisible man has accepted the illusion that Horatio Alger can be black, if he just works hard enough and does the right things.

The third episode repeats the essential elements. Fathers, both black and white, appear and keep "the nigger-boy running." Emerson, the great but unseen white father who rules Liberty Paints, a microcosm of the "heaven" of American society, has his counterpart in Lucius Brockway, the tiny black man who rules over the factory's lower depths, the inferno that keeps the factory operating. The explosion that occurs seems an immediate reaction to the quarrel between Lucius and the invisible man and to the illusory expression of friendship and understanding signified by their shaking of hands. In the end Brockway protects himself by scrambling for the stairs, and the invisible man is shot forward into a black emptiness that becomes a bath of whiteness.

The electric-shock treatment is both an instrument of castration and a mechanism for the *danse macabre*. Racist doctors joke among themselves about whether actual castration would be as effective as electric shocks, and as the invisible man's body shakes rapidly to the stimulus, executing light-ninglike patterns through space, the doctors joke about whether "they really do have rhythm" (232). Even within his fog these comments make the invisible man muderously angry, though at the same time he feels a sense of remoteness caused, he believes, by something within him that has been disconnected. The emergence of this schism of self in the invisible man is an indication of how Ras, though a more extreme example, can be both exhorter and destroyer and of how Tod, a shadow counterpart of the invisible man, can simultaneously negate his manhood and exhibit for the amusement of spectators the dancing cardboard figure metaphorically balling the jack. As Tod manipulates the figure and voices his speech, his own body and form take on aspects similar to those of the grinning doll, and he mimes Sambo, emasculated and grotesque. His castration accomplished, Tod allows himself to be shot, realizing by his own actions and out of his own deep despair the major implications of the metaphor.

Ras, Tod, and the invisible man form a trinity of sons, each reacting in different ways to the tyranny of the fathers. Ras assumes the costume of the lion and the guise of the Rastafarians to preach of redemption through separatism. (The figure of Ras in *Invisible Man* clearly needs further discussion. To my knowledge, no one has traced Ras and the cult he represents to a point in past time where in the mythology Saint Nicolas was the savior figure and Black Peter, Nicolas's counterpart. Ishmael Reed in *The Terrible Twos* explores this dimension of the myth. It does seem that at least on one allegorical level in *Invisible Man*, white Saint Nicolases and Black Peters are the fathers.) Tod is established as counterpart to Ras immediately upon Tod's introduction to the narrator. But where Ras is presented in warlike costume, Tod is characterized as typically Negro, very handsome and very black with chiseled features and kingly stature; Tod is a kind of black Billy Budd whose inability to articulate his hurts causes his death and consequent metamorphosis to savior-martyr proportions. As they do to Billy Budd, the folk rally to Tod's death, and the invisible man takes advantage of the situation both, as he says, to give Tod back his integrity and also to prove his own manhood to the Brotherhood.

As Freud clearly points out in *Totem and Taboo* (see Emerson's or his son's reading), fathers cannot tolerate potent sons. The invisible man was hired, Jack tells him, to speak, not to think, not to act on his own responsibility for anything. Ellison's use of the Cyclopes legend also echoes the theme. The Cyclopes and their brothers were imprisoned in Tartarus by their father, Uranus, for fear his sons would rebel against him. But Cronus, a Titan, with the help of his mother, Gaea, castrates Uranus. Later the Cyclopes are imprisoned by Cronus (son become ruler-father). In return for their freedom, they give Zeus, son of Cronus, the thunderbolt that helps him defeat Cronus.

The invisible man's assumption of the Rinehart guise is both a seeking for, and a hiding of, his potency. Rinehart is the heart of the matter—both rind and heart. He is the surreal paradox, the seen-unseen, the old-new, the sinner-minister, at home in a world where "only the unbelievable could be believed," where "truth was always a lie" (487). Holding within himself all possibilities, Rinehart cannot be defined or confined by absolutes and thus cannot be hurt. Recognizing no father, he avoids castration and dances to no other man's tunes.

Allusions to Hesse's *Steppenwolf* in the long and pivotal chapter 23 reinforce both theme and technique, as the invisible man first recognizes and then can begin to articulate the essential absurdity of his existence. But he is not yet his own father. He still seeks his father's women—a wife, a

girlfriend, a secretary who will be willing to talk freely about the Brotherhood. Sybil is the white woman he chooses; but he still clutches his briefcase
and he refuses to act out Sybil's rape/fantasy grounded in the American
desire for power/potency. In so doing, the invisible man aligns himself more
with the clean-cut Horatio Alger of American fictional fame than he does
with Rinehart, the trickster.

The riot that ensues is once more a choreography of violence where blacks
fight blacks in another version of the battle royal. The invisible man tells
Ras, "They want you guilty of your own murder, your own sacrifice!" (545).
Jack (and the other fathers) not only named the invisible man but in the
very instant of the naming set him running, set others like him running,
too, chasing one another like a lurid nightmare where escape is down a
manhole and freedom begins with the burning of the contents of a briefcase.
Castration/death can be avoided by recognizing that a choreographed chase
(of American origin) that circles on itself is also a merry-go-round and that
the American merry-go-round was built by black men and white men alike.

But what about women? In *Shadow and Act*, Ellison makes the point:

> Too often what is presented as the American Negro (a most complex
> example of Western Man) emerges as over-simplified clown, a beast
> or an angel. Seldom is he drawn as that sensitively focused process of
> opposites, of good and evil, of instinct and intellect, of passion and
> spirituality, which great literary art has projected as the image of man.
> Naturally, the attitude of Negroes toward this writing is one of great
> reservation.   (25–26)

Nowhere in *Invisible Man* is there a woman not characterized as
automaton—prostitute or mother. From the blond woman in the opening
scene, through the innocent and nameless black girls who dream of romantic
love and marriage, to Sybil, subsumed by fantasies of rape, to Mary, the
"good" mother, who sustains as well as destroys, the women are one-
dimensional figures playing roles in a drama written by men. Nevertheless,
there is some hidden knowledge concerning women that hovers just below
the level of the invisible man's consciousness. From the prologue where in
the deepest levels of the reefer hallucination the invisible man finds first an
old woman singing a spiritual and then a beautiful girl pleading in a voice
similar to that of his mother for control of her own naked body to the end
of the novel where he sees the hanging of the seven mannequins, a reader
today must be aware of the invisibility and impotence of women in society.
In the chapel, the thin brown girl's voice becomes a disembodied force that
seeks to enter her, "to violate her, shaking her, rocking her rhythmically,
as though it had become the source of her being, rather than the fluid web
of her own creation" (114). Miss Susie Gresham at the college is the guardian

of the young women sitting on the puritan benches. For the invisible man, however, she holds the key to something warm and vital and enduring.

Although there are some women in the Brotherhood, they all, with the possible exception of Emma, seem to be wives, secretaries, girlfriends, or hangers-on of men. Emma, Jack's mistress, acts as hostess, dispensing drinks and occasionally money. The party that takes place is clearly taking place in her richly furnished dwelling. The only woman who asks an intelligent question at a meeting of the Brotherhood is a "plain woman" (303). The invisible man's assignment to the "Woman Question" is a demotion that he understands as an outrageous joke. When he speaks to a female audience, the women respond stereotypically, with a sense of sexual excitement. The white woman who invites him to her apartment and seduces him uses all the clichés, including words like "you convey the great throbbing vitality of the movement" (402). Most of the action in the novel concerning Sybil is taken up with her attempt to get the invisible man to play the role of a brute and to pretend that he is raping her. He reasons to himself:

> But why be surprised, when that's what they hear all their lives. When it's made into a great power and they're taught to worship all types of power? With all the warnings against it, some are bound to want to try it out for themselves. The conquerors conquered. Maybe a great number secretly want it; maybe that's why they scream when it's farthest from possibility— (509)

A counterpart to Mary Rambo is the huge woman in gingham who is sitting on the top of a Borden's milk wagon and drinking beer from a barrel that is next to her. She is singing with blues timbre, holding a dipper in her hand, and bowing graciously from side to side. She drinks beer and hands it out to people, and as she does so she drops quart after quart onto the street. The body, white and naked and horribly feminine, that the invisible man thinks he sees hanging from a lamppost is counterpart to the naked body of the platinum blond in the opening scene and to the naked body of Sybil (511). On the belly of one is an American flag, on the belly of the other, written in lipstick, are the words:

SYBIL, YOU WERE RAPED
BY
SANTA CLAUS
SURPRISE

The body hanging from a lamppost becomes in montage pattern seven mannequins—"Hairless, bald and sterilely feminine" (543). The only woman acting with any semblance of real power is Trueblood's wife, who takes on herself the roles of judge, jury, and executioner but who is finally unable to carry out her sentence. Later she is corrupted when she accepts items of material value offered her by false fathers.

It is, of course, possible that Ellison presents through the invisible man's narration stereotypes of women in an effort to call attention to the stereotypes. It is possible that Ellison underlines female invisibility by presenting women as only fractions of a whole, dismembered parts, as it were. Buried deep in the invisible man's subconscious is the image of his grandmother trying to function in a patriarchal American society. Perhaps when he emerges from his hole, he will be able to bring her to the level of consciousness and thus begin the process of making her and all women as visible as men.

SAMPLE STUDY GUIDES

Questions for Discussion

James R. Andreas

1. Comment briefly on the significance of the new introduction to the novel. Does it surprise you that the book was originally conceived as a war novel? What varieties of fascism remain to be confronted at home? Why does Ellison tell us he adopted a comic tone in his novel?

2. What sense do you make of the title and of the epigraphs to the novel?

3. Why does Ellison begin his novel at the conclusion? What specifically do you learn of the hero's condition at the conclusion? What sense do you make of the hero's pastimes and memories? What has he retained from his "battles"? Why does the hero fight with the white man at the beginning of the prologue? What do you make of the Monopolated Light Company? What is the significance of the sermon and the questioning of the mother?

4. Discuss the significance of the battle royal. What structure or pattern does it set up for the remaining adventures of the novel? Why is the hero continually chosen "to represent his race"? How is the woman treated in the scene? Why is each episode in the novel punctuated or climaxed by a "battle royal" or a fight?

5. Why are the white elders of the community so impressed with the hero? Do they really believe in humility and nonviolence, or even in

the "social responsibility" they expect the hero to address in his vale-
dictory speech?

6. What advice does the grandfather supply the hero? Why is the hero
    left nameless throughout the novel?

7. Keep track of the hero's dreams and of the "dreams" others would
    impose on the hero. Why does the grandfather level the curse on him:
    "Keep this nigger running?"

8. What is the function of the black campus? What harsh realities does
    it protect black and white leadership from perceiving? How is the
    Founder characterized? Why has Bledsoe been hired? Why does he
    drive a "cream-colored wife" around in his "cream-colored Cadillac"?
    What is Norton's interest in the school? Discuss the function of True-
    blood. Is the oedipal problem that is discussed in this chapter a phe-
    nomenon limited to the black community? Why does Norton identify
    so fully with Trueblood? What sexual forms does racism take in Amer-
    ican history? What kinds of speakers do the trustees invite to the
    campus? Discuss Homer Barbee's speech in detail. Why is he blind
    and what myth of the Founder does he reconstruct? Discuss the influ-
    ence of Booker T. Washington's philosophy on the college policy re-
    garding the education of black youth. Why is the visit to the Golden
    Day such a catastrophe for the hero—and for Norton?

9. Discuss the role of the vets in the story. Why does the "moon-mad
    mockingbird" reappear in the imagery of Ellison from time to time?
    How and why metaphorically does it flip its tail at the Founder? Com-
    pare and contrast the function of these vets with the accommodation
    to white domination practiced by a Bledsoe or a Barbee.

10. Why does the hero begin in a small southern town and then move
    north ultimately only to drop out of society altogether? Comment on
    the hero's political progress in the novel. How do his perceptions of
    social, racial, and political problems develop throughout the novel?
    What brings him to party prominence later on and how does he even-
    tually fail Brother Jack? Why have black Americans inevitably exper-
    imented with left-wing politics?

11. Discuss the theme of leadership in *Invisible Man*. Why is the hero
    targeted as a leader by the various organizations to which he belongs
    and to whom he pays allegiance—if only temporarily?

12. Examine two or three of the speeches of the hero. How does speech (i.e., language) clarify the hero's perceptions of himself and the institutions that dominate his everyday actions? Examine two or three of his speeches in thematic and rhetorical detail. For instance, discuss the eviction speech as a model for the hero's other speeches. With what premise does he begin and to what conclusion does his logic lead him? How is his attitude toward "social responsibility" modified by this particular speech?

13. How and why does the hero play with words, with words like *yam* ("I am what I am") and names like Rinehart (rind and heart)? What does he make of *nigger* and *trigger* in his funeral speech for Tod Clifton? In other words, what does his knowledge of language teach him? From whom does he learn these street lessons? Give instances of the derivation of current vocabulary from such straightforward street language.

14. Compare and contrast the hero, Oedipus, and Hamlet as literary characters or protagonists. Does the hero consider himself a hero? Why not? Does Hamlet? Does Oedipus? When Oedipus does, what sort of trouble does he get into?

15. Comment on the theme of liberty in the novel and discuss the episode at Liberty Paint as an allegory of the hero's condition. Why does the hero come into conflict with the union at this point? What has Emerson learned from his namesake? What didn't he learn? Why would he play Huck to the hero's nigger Jim? What problems does Emerson have with his own father?

16. Discuss the relationship of the hero to the white "masters" in the novel: Norton, Emerson, and Brother Jack. How do they intend to control his destiny and how would they manipulate him to control the destiny of his race? What favors does the hero think have been done for him in the long run by Norton, Bledsoe, Emerson, and Brother Jack? In fact, how is it that the hero can turn defeat into success in instance after instance?

17. Are certain historic black leaders—such as Marcus Garvey, Booker T. Washington, W. E. B. Du Bois, and Frederick Douglass—represented directly or indirectly by the various leaders depicted in the novel? How does Ras co-opt the hero just as surely as do the white paternalists the hero endorses? Discuss Ras's philosophy of black nationalism and compare it with the ideas of Marcus Garvey, Elijah Mohammed, and Malcolm X.

18.   What sort of freedom does Rinehart offer the hero? Why is Rinehart the quintessentially invisible man? How does the hero cultivate his newfound invisibility as a strategy for dodging compromise and accommodation?

19.   Discuss the relationship of the hero to the white "mistresses" in the novel: the stripper, the wife of the brother, and Sybil. In contrast, what does the hero learn from Mary Rambo? How is she different from the white women he comes into contact with? How does Gwen manipulate him? What do the hero's relationships have to do with Tod Clifton's dancing Sambo dolls? Are there other symbols of the hero's puppetlike behavior in the novel?

20.   How is the hero's identity molded by the security and responsibility of corporate life? What constitutes medical treatment and "sanity" in the corporate world? Discuss the scene in the company hospital in detail. What does Brer Rabbit have to do with the hero? Discuss the derivation of the Uncle Remus stories from African myth. Why does the hero fail repeatedly in corporate and party contexts? Why does he fail to conform to the social demands that would infringe on his rights to freedom and the pursuit of happiness?

21.   Why does the hero quarrel with Brother Jack? What does he learn from the experiences of Tarp and Tod Clifton? Why do puppets and dolls (e.g., the African bank) play such an important symbolic role in the novel? Discuss the varieties of servitude in the novel.

22.   What does Ellison seem to be saying about the causes of periodic racial riots in American life? Why does Ras whip up riot sentiments? What do conditions in the ghetto have to do with these riots? Discuss several traditional and recent examples of such riots in American history. How does the riot break out? How does the hero use the possessions gathered in his briefcase to defend himself in this riot, particularly against Ras?

23.   Comment on the final dream of the hero where all the major characters reassemble to discuss the hero's progress—or regress. What do you make of the blinding/castration theme in the dream? Is he castrated or blinded or both? What illusions is he free of? How does the hero interpret his dream?

24.   Discuss the hero's decision to hibernate from the perspective of the end of the novel. What promise for release and renewal is made?

Morals and Values

Susan Resneck Parr

General Questions

1. How possible is it for individuals to transcend their personal and cultural histories? To what degree do those histories blind them to the realities of the present and thus make them unable to "see" or even to define the moral choices available to them?

2. Do people genuinely have the free will to act on the moral choices they make?

3. What in fact is moral choice? What is a "socially responsible" role?

4. Even if we assume that a given individual has sight, free will, and a commitment to acting in a socially responsible way, how much can any individual affect either the social order or social values?

5. What is the appropriate balance between an individual's personal needs and that individual's obligation to society or to groups within society?

6. Does power corrupt?

7. Is personal exile an appropriate response to social injustice?

8. What is the relation between oppression and violence?

9. Is the creation of a work of art sufficient as a socially responsible act? In discussing this question, consider the impact on history of both Thoreau's refusal to pay his poll tax and his writing "Civil Disobedience."

10. Is *Invisible Man* a superior work of art, as many of its readers argue, because it has universal implications, or is it flawed, as others insist, because it is not specifically enough a "protest novel" or a novel that does justice to the Afro-American experience?

Questions on Invisible Man

1. Is the invisible man evolving to a new moral consciousness throughout the novel? What is the significance of his refusal to embrace a specific

137

plan of action? Pay particular attention here to the prologue and the epilogue.

2. How does the blindness-sight imagery function in terms of the invisibility-visibility motif?

3. What is the function of the references to Eden and of the many serpentine images in the novel?

4. Discuss Ellison's debts to Freud, the existentialists, and Marx. In this connection, note the references to the invisible man as part of a machine, as mechanical and robotlike.

5. In some ways, *Invisible Man* parodies aspects of Booker T. Washington's *Up from Slavery*. Discuss.

6. Discuss the thematic significance of the various surrealistic scenes, such as the episode in the Golden Day and the Harlem riots, in terms of the invisible man's growing self-knowledge.

7. What are the ingredients of political satire, in terms of both imagery and action, in the Liberty Paint factory episode?

PARTICIPANTS IN SURVEY OF ELLISON INSTRUCTORS AND CONTRIBUTORS TO THE VOLUME

The following scholars and teachers contributed essays or participated in the survey of approaches to teaching *Invisible Man* that preceded preparation of this book or both. Their assistance, support, and patience made the volume possible.

James R. Andreas, Drury College; Robert H. Bell, Williams College; Jonathan Bishop, Cornell University; Richard Bizot, University of North Florida; Nicholas Canaday, Louisiana State University, Baton Rouge; Arlene L. Clift, Fisk University; John Cooke, University of New Orleans; Leonard Deutsch, Marshall University; Rudolf F. Dietze, Universitat Erlangen-Nurnberg; Fidelis Doyle, Villanova University; William Ferris, University of Mississippi; Robert E. Fleming, University of New Mexico; Henry Louis Gates, Jr., Cornell University; L. M. Grow, College of the Bahamas; Diane S. Isaacs, University of Minnesota, Twin Cities; Sharon Adele Jessee, Rutgers University, New Brunswick; Madeleine Kisner, Kansas Newman College; Lynne Layton, Boston University; Eleanor Lyons, Indiana University of South Bend; Diane Matza, Utica College, Syracuse University; Loren R. McKeown, Cameron University; R. Baxter Miller, University of Tennessee, Knoxville; Wilson J. Moses, Brown University; Neil Nakadate, Iowa State University; Louis Oldani, Rockhurst College; Susan Resneck Parr, University of Tulsa; John M. Reilly, State University of New York, Albany; Stewart Rodnon, Rider College; Mary Rohrberger, Oklahoma State University; Mariann Russell, Sacred Heart University; Pancho Savery, University of Massachusetts, Boston; Edith Schor, Bronx Community College, City University of New York; Walter Slatoff, Cornell University; Christopher Sten, George Washington University; Cushing Strout, Cornell University; Gordon O. Taylor, University of Tulsa; David L. Vanderwerken, Texas Christian University; James E. Walton, Mount Union College.

WORKS CITED

Aaron, Daniel. *Writers on the Left.* 1961. New preface. New York: Oxford UP, 1977.

Allen, Michael. "Some Examples of Faulknerian Rhetoric in Ellison's *Invisible Man.*" Bigsby, *Black American Writer* 143–51.

Appignanesi, Richard, and Oscar Zarate. *Lenin for Beginners.* Rev. ed. New York: Pantheon, 1978.

Armstrong, Louis. "Buddy Bolden's Blues." Rec. 11 Sept. 1946. *New Orleans: Original Soundtrack.* Giants of Jazz, GOJ-1025, 1983.

———. "Potato Head Blues." Rec. 10 May 1927. *Giants of Jazz: Louis Armstrong.* Time-Life, STL-J01 P3 14674, 1978.

———. "(What Did I Do to Be So) Black and Blue." Rec. 22 July 1929. *Giants of Jazz: Louis Armstrong.* Time-Life, STL-J01 P3 14674, 1978.

———. "(What Did I Do to Be So) Black and Blue." *Louis Armstrong's Greatest Hits.* Columbia, CS 9438, 1967.

Baker, Houston A., Jr. *Blues, Ideology, and Afro-American Literature: A Vernacular Theory.* Chicago: U of Chicago P, 1984.

———. "Critical Change and Blues Continuity: An Essay on the Criticism of Larry Neal." *Callaloo* 8 (1985): 70–84.

———. "A Forgotten Prototype: *The Autobiography of an Ex-Colored Man* and *Invisible Man.*" *Singers of Daybreak: Studies in Black American Literature.* By Baker. Washington: Howard UP, 1974. 17–31.

———. *The Journey Back: Issues in Black Literature and Criticism.* Chicago: U of Chicago P, 1980.

Baldwin, James. *The Fire Next Time.* New York: Dial, 1963.

———. *Notes of a Native Son.* Boston: Beacon, 1955.

Baraka, Amiri. *Blues People: Negro Music in White America.* New York: Morrow, 1963.

Barrett, Leonard. *The Rastafarians: Sounds of Cultural Dissonance.* Boston: Beacon, 1977.

Barrett, William. *Irrational Man: A Study in Existential Philosophy.* Garden City: Doubleday, 1958.

———. *Time of Need: Forms of Imagination in the Twentieth Century.* New York: Harper, 1972.

Basie, Count. "Harvard Blues." With Jimmy Rushing. Rec. 17 Nov. 1941. *Giants of Jazz: Count Basie.* Time-Life, STL-J22 P3 15743, 1982.

Bateson, Gregory. *Steps to an Ecology of Mind.* San Francisco: Chandler, 1972.

Baumbach, Jonathan. "Nightmare of a Native Son: Ellison's *Invisible Man.*" *The Landscape of Nightmare.* By Baumbach. New York: New York UP, 1965. 68–86.

Benston, Kimberly. "Ellison, Baraka, and the Faces of Tradition." *Boundary 2* 6 (Winter 1978): 333–54.

———, ed. *Speaking for You: The Vision of Ralph Ellison*. Washington: Howard UP, 1987.

Bigsby, C. W. E., ed. *The Black American Writer*. Vol. 1. 1969. Baltimore: Penguin, 1971.

———. "From Protest to Paradox: The Black Writer at Mid Century." *The Fifties: Fiction, Poetry, Drama*. Ed. Warren French. Deland: Everett/Edwards, 1970. 217–40.

Black World 20 (Dec. 1970). Special Ellison issue.

Blake, Susan L. "Ritual and Rationalization: Black Folklore in the Works of Ralph Ellison." *PMLA* 94 (1979): 121–36.

Bluestein, Gene. *The Voice of the Folk*. Amherst: U of Massachusetts P, 1972.

Bone, Robert A. *The Negro Novel in America*. Rev. ed. New Haven: Yale UP, 1965.

Boot, Adrian, and Vivien Goldman. *Bob Marley: Soul Rebel–Natural Mystic*. 1981. New York: St. Martin's, 1982.

Boskin, Joseph. "The Life and Death of Sambo: Overview of an Historical Hang-up." *Journal of Popular Culture* 4 (1971): 647–57.

Brée, Germaine. *Camus and Sartre: Crisis and Commitment*. New York: Dell, 1972.

Breisach, Ernst. *Introduction to Modern Existentialism*. New York: Grove, 1962.

Broderick, Francis L. W. E. B. *DuBois: Negro Leader in a Time of Crisis*. Stanford: Stanford UP, 1959.

Brooks, Gwendolyn. *The World of Gwendolyn Brooks*. New York: Harper, 1971.

Brown, Claude. *Manchild in the Promised Land*. New York: Macmillan, 1965.

Brown, Lloyd W. "Black Entitles: Names as Symbols in Afro-American Literature." *Studies in Black Literature* 1.1 (1970): 16–44.

———. "Ralph Ellison's Exhorters: The Role of Rhetoric in *Invisible Man*." *CLA Journal* 13 (1970): 289–303.

Bryant, Jerry H. "Wright, Ellison, Baldwin: Exorcising the Demon." *Phylon* 37 (1977): 174–88.

Butler, Robert J. "Dante's *Inferno* and Ellison's *Invisible Man*: A Study in Literary Continuity." *CLA Journal* 28 (1984): 57–77.

Callahan, John. "Democracy and the Pursuit of Narrative." *Carleton Miscellany* 18 (1980): 51–68.

———. "The Historical Frequencies of Ralph Ellison." *Chant of Saints: A Gathering of Afro-American Literature, Art, and Scholarship*. Ed. Michael S. Harper and Robert B. Stepto. Urbana: U of Illinois P, 1979. 33–52.

Cannon, Steve, Lenox Raphael, and James Thompson. " 'A Very Stern Discipline': An Interview with Ralph Ellison." *Harper's* Mar. 1967: 76–95.

Carleton Miscellany 18 (1980). Special Ellison issue.

Chapman, Abraham, ed. *Black Voices: An Anthology of Afro-American Literature*. New York: Mentor–NAL, 1968.

Chaucer, Geoffrey. *The Complete Poetry and Prose*. Ed. John H. Fisher. New York: Holt, 1977.

Christian, Barbara. "Ralph Ellison: A Critical Study." *Black Expression: Essays by and about Black Americans in the Creative Arts*. Ed. Addison Gayle, Jr. New York: Weybright, 1969. 353–65.

Christian, Charlie. *Solo Flight: The Genius of Charlie Christian*. Columbia Records, CG 30779, 1972.

CLA Journal 13 (1970). Special Ellison issue.

Clarke, John Henrik, ed. *Harlem: A Community in Transition*. New York: Citadel, 1969.

———, ed. *Marcus Garvey and the Vision of Africa*. New York: Vintage, 1974.

———. "The Visible Dimension of *Invisible Man*." *Black World* 20 (Dec. 1970): 27–30.

Cleaver, Eldridge. *Soul on Ice*. New York: McGraw, 1968.

Clipper, Lawrence J. "Folkloric and Mythic Elements in *Invisible Man*." *CLA Journal* 13 (1970): 229–41.

Collier, Eugenia W. "Dimensions of Alienation in Two Black American and Caribbean Novels." *Phylon* 43 (1982): 46–56.

———. "The Nightmare Truth of an Invisible Man." *Black World* 20 (Dec. 1970), 12–19.

Conrad, Joseph. *Lord Jim*. New York: Norton, 1968.

Cooke, Michael G. *Afro-American Literature in the Twentieth Century: The Achievement of Intimacy*. New Haven: Yale UP, 1984.

———, ed. *Modern Black Novelists: A Collection of Critical Essays*. Englewood Cliffs: Prentice, 1971.

Covo, Jacqueline. *The Blinking Eye: Ralph Waldo Ellison and His American, French, German and Italian Critics, 1952–1971*. Metuchen: Scarecrow, 1974.

Cox, Oliver C. *Caste, Class, and Race: A Study in Social Dynamics*. Garden City: Doubleday, 1948.

Cronon, E. David. *Black Moses: The Story of Marcus Garvey and the Universal Negro Improvement Association*. 2nd ed. Madison: U of Wisconsin P, 1969.

Crossman, Richard, ed. *The God Who Failed*. 1950. New York: Bantam, 1952.

Cruse, Harold. *The Crisis of the Negro Intellectual*. New York: Morrow, 1967.

Davis, Arthur P. *From the Dark Tower: Afro-American Writers 1900–1960*. Washington: Howard UP, 1974.

Davis, Stephen. *Bob Marley*. Garden City: Doubleday, 1985.

Davis, Stephen, and Peter Simon. *Reggae Bloodlines: In Search of the Music and Culture of Jamaica*. 1977. Rev. ed. New York: Anchor-Doubleday, 1979.

———. *Reggae International*. New York: Rogner, 1982.

Deutsch, Leonard J. "Ralph Waldo Ellison." *Dictionary of Literary Biography: Vol. 2: American Novelists since World War II*. Detroit: Gale, 1978. 136–41.

———. "Ralph Waldo Ellison and Ralph Waldo Emerson: A Shared Moral Vision." *CLA Journal* 16 (1972): 159–78.

———. "The Waste Land in Ellison's *Invisible Man*." *Notes on Contemporary Literature* 7.6 (1977): 5–6.

Dostoevsky, Fyodor. Notes from Underground *and* The Grand Inquisitor. 1864, 1880. Trans. Constance Garnett. Rev. and ed. Ralph E. Matlaw. New York: Dutton, 1960.

———. *The Brothers Karamazov*. 1880. Trans. Constance Garnett. Rev. and ed. Ralph E. Matlaw. New York: Norton, 1976.

Douglass, Frederick. *The Life and Times of Frederick Douglass*. 1881. Rev. ed. 1892. New York: Bonanza-Crowell, 1962.

———. *My Bondage and My Freedom*. 1855. New York: Dover, 1969.

———. *Narrative of the Life of Frederick Douglass, an American Slave, Written by Himself*. 1845. New York: Signet-NAL, 1968.

Drake, St. Clair. *The Redemption of Africa and Black Religion*. Chicago: Third World, 1970.

Du Bois, W. E. B. *The Souls of Black Folk*. 1903. New York: Fawcett, 1961.

Eliot, T. S. *The Complete Poems and Plays, 1909–1950*. New York: Harcourt, 1952.

Ellenberger, Henri F. *The Discovery of the Unconscious: The History and Evolution of Dynamic Psychiatry*. New York: Basic, 1970.

Ellison, Ralph. "Editorial Comment." *Negro Quarterly* (Winter 1934): 300.

———. *Going to the Territory*. New York: Random, 1986.

———. Introduction. *Invisible Man*. New York: Random, 1982. ix–xxi.

———. *Invisible Man*. 1952. New York: Vintage, 1972.

———. "Out of the Hospital and under the Bar." *Soon, One Morning: New Writing by American Negroes 1940–1962*. Ed. Herbert Hill. New York: Knopf, 1963. 242–90.

———. *Shadow and Act*. 1964. New York: Vintage, 1972.

———. "Stormy Weather." *New Masses* 24 Sept. 1940: 20–21.

———. "The Uses of History in Fiction." *Southern Literary Journal* 1.2 (1969): 57–90.

Emerson, Ralph Waldo. "The American Scholar." *Complete Works* 1: 81–115.

———. "The Comic." *Complete Works* 8: 155–74.

———. *The Complete Works of Ralph Waldo Emerson*. Ed. Edward Waldo Emerson. 12 vols. Boston: Houghton, 1903–04.

———. *Selections from Ralph Waldo Emerson*. Ed. Stephen E. Whicher. Boston: Houghton, 1960.

———. "Self-Reliance." *Essays: First Series*. Vol. 2 of *The Collected Works of Ralph Waldo Emerson*. Ed. Alfred R. Ferguson, Jean Ferguson Carr, and Joseph Slater. Cambridge: Belknap–Harvard UP, 1979. 25–51.

Erikson, Erik. "Identity, Psychosocial." *International Encyclopedia of the Social Sciences.* New York: Macmillan, 1968.

———. *Identity: Youth and Crisis.* New York: Norton, 1968.

Essien-Udom, E. U. "The Nationalist Movements of Harlem." Clarke, *Harlem* 97–104.

Fanon, Frantz. *The Wretched of the Earth.* 1961. Trans. Constance Farrington. New York: Grove, 1968.

Faristzaddi, Millard. *Itations of Jamaica and I Rastafari.* New York: Rogner, 1982.

Fass, Barbara. "Rejection of Paternalism: Hawthorne's 'My Kinsman Major Molineux' and Ellison's *Invisible Man.*" *CLA Journal* 15 (1971): 171–96.

Fauset, Arthur H. *Black Gods of the Metropolis.* 1944. Philadelphia: U of Pennsylvania P, 1971.

Fischer, Russell G. "*Invisible Man* as History." *CLA Journal* 17 (1974): 338–67.

Fitzgerald, F. Scott. *The Great Gatsby.* 1925. New York: Scribner's, 1970.

Fleming, Robert E. "Contemporary Themes in Johnson's *Autobiography of an Ex-Colored Man.*" *Negro American Literature Forum* 4 (Winter 1970): 120–24.

Ford, Nick Aaron. "The Ambivalence of Ralph Ellison." *Black World* 20 (Dec. 1970): 5–9.

Forrest, Leon. "A Conversation with Ralph Ellison." *Muhammad Speaks* 15 Dec. 1972: 29–31.

———. "Racial History as a Clue to the Action in *Invisible Man.*" *Muhammad Speaks* 15 Sept. 1972: 28–30.

Fowles, John. *The Aristos.* 1964. New York: Plume-NAL, 1975.

Frank, Joseph. "Ralph Ellison and a Literary 'Ancestor': Dostoevsky." *New Criterion* 2.1 (1983): 11–21.

Franklin, Benjamin. *The Autobiography of Benjamin Franklin.* New York: Modern Library–Random, 1981.

Franklin, John Hope. *From Slavery to Freedom: A History of Negro Americans.* 3rd ed. New York: Knopf, 1967.

———, ed. *Three Negro Classics.* New York: Avon, 1965.

Franklin, John Hope, and Isidore Starr, eds. *The Negro in Twentieth Century America.* New York: Random, 1967.

Frazier, E. Franklin. *Black Bourgeoisie.* Glencoe: Free, 1957.

Freud, Sigmund. *Totem and Taboo: Some Points of Agreement between the Mental Lives of Savages and Neurotics.* 1913. Trans. James Strachey. New York: Norton, 1950.

Garvey, Marcus. *Philosophy and Opinions of Marcus Garvey.* Ed. Amy Jacques-Garvey. 2 vols. 1923, 1925. New York: Atheneum, 1969.

Gates, Henry Louis, Jr. "The Blackness of Blackness: A Critique of the Sign and the Signifying Monkey." *Black Literature and Literary Theory.* Ed. Gates. New York: Methuen, 1984. 285–321.

Gayle, Addison, Jr., ed. *The Black Aesthetic.* Garden City: Doubleday, 1971.

Geller, Allen. "An Interview with Ralph Ellison." Bigsby, *Black American Writer* 153–68.

Gibson, Donald B. "Ralph Ellison and James Baldwin." *The Politics of Twentieth-Century Novelists.* Ed. George A. Panichas. New York: Crowell, 1974. 307–20.

Girard, René. "Perilous Balance: A Comic Hypothesis." *Modern Language Notes* 87 (1977): 811–26.

Girson, Rochelle. "Sidelights on Invisibility." *Saturday Review* 14 Mar. 1953: 20 + .

Goede, William. "On Lower Frequencies: The Buried Men in Wright and Ellison." *Modern Fiction Studies* 15 (1969): 483–501.

Gordon, Eugene. "Social and Political Problems of the Negro Writer." *American Writers' Congress.* Ed. Henry Hurt. New York: International, 1935. 141–45.

Gottesman, Ronald, ed. *The Merrill Studies in* Invisible Man. Columbus: Merrill, 1971.

Gramsci, Antonio. *Selections from the Prison Notebooks of Antonio Gramsci.* Trans. and ed. Quintin Hoare and Geoffrey Nowell Smith. New York: International, 1971.

Griffin, Edward M. "Notes from a Clean, Well-Lighted Place: Ralph Ellison's *Invisible Man.*" *Twentieth Century Literature* 15 (1969): 129–44.

Griffin, John Howard. *Black like Me.* Boston: Houghton, 1961.

Griffiths, Trevor. *Occupations.* Rev. ed. London: Faber, 1980.

Hall, Calvin S. *A Primer of Freudian Psychology.* New York: Mentor-World, 1954.

Harding, Vincent. "Black Reflections on the Cultural Ramifications of Black Identity." *Black Books Bulletin* Winter 1972: 4–10.

Harris, Trudier. "Ellison's 'Peter Wheatstraw': His Basis in Black Folk Tradition." *Mississippi Folklore Register* 9 (1975): 117–26.

Hassan, Ihab. *Radical Innocence: Studies in the Contemporary American Novel.* Princeton: Princeton UP, 1961.

Heermance, J. N. "A White Critic's Viewpoint: The Modern Negro Novel." *Negro Digest* 13 (May 1965): 66–76.

Herndon, Angelo. *Let Me Live.* 1937. New York: Arno–New York Times, 1969.

Hersey, John, ed. *Ralph Ellison: A Collection of Critical Essays.* Englewood Cliffs: Prentice, 1970.

Hill, Herbert, ed. *Anger and Beyond: The Negro Writer in the United States.* New York: Harper, 1966.

Hot Tuna. *Hot Tuna.* RCA, LSP-4353, 1970.

Howe, Irving. *A World More Attractive.* New York: Horizon, 1963.

Huggins, Nathan Irvin. *Harlem Renaissance.* New York: Oxford UP, 1971.

———. *Slave and Citizen: The Life of Frederick Douglass.* Boston: Little, 1980.

Hughes, Langston, and Arna Bontemps, eds. *The Book of Negro Folklore.* New York: Dodd, 1958.

Hurston, Zora Neale. *Their Eyes Were Watching God.* 1937. Urbana: U of Illinois P, 1978.

Hurt, John. *The Best of Mississippi John Hurt.* Rec. 15 Apr. 1965. Vanguard, VSD 19/20.

Hyman, Stanley Edgar. *The Promised End.* New York: World, 1963.

Jacques-Garvey, Amy. *Garvey and Garveyism.* 1963. New York: Collier, 1970.

Jahn, Janheinz. *Muntu: An Outline of the New African Culture.* 1958. Trans. Marjorie Grene. New York: Grove, 1961.

Jemie, Onwuchekwa. *Langston Hughes: An Introduction to the Poetry.* New York: Columbia UP, 1976.

Johnson, Abby Arthur. "Birds of Passage: Flight Imagery in *Invisible Man.*" *Studies in the Twentieth Century* 14 (Fall 1974): 91–104.

Johnson, James Weldon. *The Autobiography of an Ex-Colored Man.* Franklin, *Three Negro Classics* 391–511.

Joyce, James. *A Portrait of the Artist as a Young Man.* 1916. New York: Viking, 1956.

Kaufmann, Walter, ed. and trans. *Existentialism from Dostoevsky to Sartre.* Cleveland: Meridian-World, 1956.

Kazin, Alfred. *Bright Book of Life: American Novelists and Storytellers from Hemingway to Mailer.* 1973. New York: Dell, 1974.

Kern, Edith. *The Absolute Comic.* New York: Columbia UP, 1980.

Kierkegaard, Søren. *Concluding Unscientific Postscript.* 1846. Trans. David F. Swenson and Walter Lowrie. Princeton: Princeton UP, 1941.

Kirst, E. M. "A Langian Analysis of Blackness in Ralph Ellison's *Invisible Man.*" *Studies in Black American Literature* 7.2 (1976): 19–34.

Klotman, Phyllis R. "The Running Man as Metaphor in Ellison's *Invisible Man.*" *CLA Journal* 13 (1970): 277–88.

Lenin, V. I. *Essential Works of Lenin.* Ed. Henry M. Christman. New York: Bantam, 1966.

Lewis, David Levering. *When Harlem Was in Vogue.* New York: Knopf, 1981.

Lewis, R. W. B. *The American Adam: Innocence, Tragedy, and Tradition in the Nineteenth Century.* Chicago: U of Chicago P, 1958.

Lieber, Todd M. "Ralph Ellison and the Metaphor of Invisibility in Black Literary Tradition." *American Quarterly* 24 (1972): 86–100.

Lieberman, Marcia R. "Moral Innocents: Ellison's *Invisible Man* and *Candide.*" *CLA Journal* 15 (1971): 64–79.

List, Robert. *Dedalus in Harlem: The Joyce-Ellison Connection.* Washington: UP of America, 1982.

Locke, Alain, ed. *The New Negro.* 1925. New York: Atheneum, 1970.

Lovejoy, A. O. *Essays in the History of Ideas.* Baltimore: Johns Hopkins UP, 1948.

Major, Clarence. *Dictionary of Afro-American Slang.* New York: International, 1970.

Malcolm X. *The Autobiography of Malcolm X.* New York: Grove, 1965.

Malraux, André. *Days of Wrath*. 1935. Trans. Haakon M. Chevalier. New York: Random, 1936.

———. *Man's Fate*. 1933. Trans. Haakon M. Chevalier. 1934. New York: Random, 1961.

———. *Man's Hope*. 1937. Trans. Stuart Gilbert and Alastair Macdonald. 1938. New York: Grove, 1979.

———. *The Voices of Silence*. 1951. Trans. Stuart Gilbert. 1953. Princeton: Princeton UP, 1978.

Mannheim, Karl. *Ideology and Utopia: An Introduction to the Sociology of Knowledge*. 1936. Trans. Lewis Wirth and Edward Shils. New York: Harcourt, 1964.

McMichael, George, ed. *Anthology of American Literature*. Vol. 2. 3rd ed. New York: Macmillan, 1985.

McPherson, James Alan. "Indivisible Man." Interview with Ralph Ellison. *Atlantic* Dec. 1970: 45–60.

Meier, August, and Elliott M. Rudwick. *From Plantation to Ghetto: An Interpretive History of American Negroes*. New York: Hill, 1966.

Melville, Herman. *The Confidence-Man: His Masquerade*. 1857. Ed. H. Bruce Franklin. Indianapolis: Bobbs, 1967.

———. *Moby-Dick*. 1851. Ed. Harrison Hayford and Hershel Parker. New York: Norton, 1967.

———. *Melville's* Benito Cereno: *A Text for Guided Research*. Ed. John P. Runden. Boston: Heath, 1965.

Merton, Robert K. *Social Theory and Social Structure*. New York: Macmillan, 1965.

Moore, Richard B. "Africa Conscious Harlem." Clarke, *Harlem* 77–96.

Morton, Jelly Roll. "Buddy Bolden's Blues." Rec. 14 Sept. 1939. *Giants of Jazz: Jelly Roll Morton*. Time-Life, STLJ-5007, 1979.

Moses, Wilson J. *Black Messiahs and Uncle Toms*. University Park: Pennsylvania State UP, 1978.

———. "The Poetics of Ethiopianism: W. E. B. Du Bois and Literary Black Nationalism." *American Literature* 47 (1975): 411–26.

Mullahy, Patrick. *Oedipus: Myth and Complex; A Review of Psychoanalytic Theory*. 1948. New York: Grove, 1955.

Murray, Albert. *The Hero and the Blues*. Columbia: U of Missouri P, 1973.

———. *The Omni-Americans: New Perspectives on Black Experience and American Culture*. 1970. New York: Avon, 1971.

———. *South to a Very Old Place*. New York: McGraw, 1971.

———. *Stomping the Blues*. New York: McGraw, 1976.

———. *Train Whistle Guitar*. New York: McGraw, 1974.

Naison, Mark. *Communists in Harlem during the Depression*. Urbana: U of Illinois P, 1983.

Nash, R. W. "Stereotypes and Social Types in Ellison's *Invisible Man.*" *Sociological Quarterly* 6 (Autumn 1965): 349–60.

Neal, Larry. "Ellison's Zoot Suit." Hersey 58–79.

———. "The Ethos of the Blues." *Black Scholar* 3 (Summer 1972): 42–48.

Nicholas, Tracy, and Bill Sparrow. *Rastafari: A Way of Life.* Garden City: Anchor-Doubleday, 1979.

Oates, Joyce Carol. *Them.* New York: Vanguard, 1969.

O'Brien, John. "Ralph Ellison." *Interviews with Ten Black Writers.* By O'Brien. New York: Liveright, 1973. 63–77.

O'Meally, Robert G. *The Craft of Ralph Ellison.* Cambridge: Harvard UP, 1980.

———. "Riffs and Rituals: Folklore in the Work of Ralph Ellison." *Afro-American Literature: The Reconstruction of Instruction.* Ed. Dexter Fisher and Robert B. Stepto. New York: MLA, 1979. 153–69.

———. "The Rules of Magic: Hemingway as Ellison's 'Ancestor.' " *Southern Review* 21 (1985): 751–69.

Ottley, Roi. *New World A-Coming.* 1943. New York: Arno–New York Times, 1968.

Peyre, Henri. Introduction. *The Age of Reason.* By Jean-Paul Sartre. 1945. Trans. Eric Sutton. 1947. New York: Bantam, 1968. v–xxxvi.

Pockell, Leslie, ed. "Tomorrow's Classics: Forty Well-Known Creators, Critics, and Connoisseurs of High and Pop Art Speculate on Which Modern Works Will Endure." *Avant Garde* 6 (Jan. 1969): 28–31.

Rampersad, Arnold. *The Art and Imagination of W. E. B. DuBois.* Cambridge: Harvard UP, 1976.

Redding, J. Saunders. *No Day of Triumph.* New York: Harper, 1942.

———. *Stranger and Alone.* New York: Harcourt, 1950.

———. *They Came in Chains: Americans from Africa.* Rev. ed. Philadelphia: Lippincott, 1973.

Reed, Ishmael. *The Terrible Twos.* New York: St. Martin's, 1982.

Reed, Ishmael, Quincy Troupe, and Steve Cannon. "The Essential Ellison." *Y'Bird* 1 (1978): 126–59.

Reid, Ira De A. "Negro Movements and Messiahs, 1900–1949." *Phylon* 9 (1949): 362–75.

Reilly, John M., ed. *Twentieth Century Interpretations of* Invisible Man. Englewood Cliffs: Prentice, 1970.

Rodnon, Stewart. "*The Adventures of Huckleberry Finn* and *Invisible Man*: Thematic and Structural Comparisons." *Negro American Literature Forum* 4 (1970): 45–51.

———. "Henry Adams and Ralph Ellison: Transcending Tragedy." *Studies in the Humanities* 3 (1973): 1–7.

Rushing, Jimmy. "Boogie Woogie." "How Long Blues." *The Essential Jimmy Rushing.* Vanguard, VSD 65/66, 1974.

Sanders, Archie D. "Odysseus in Black: An Analysis of the Structure of *Invisible Man.*" *CLA Journal* 13 (1970): 217–28.

Sartre, Jean-Paul. *Critique of Dialectical Reason.* 1960. Trans. Alan Sheridan-Smith. 1976. London: Verso, 1982.

———. *Existentialism and Human Emotions.* Trans. Bernard Frechtman and Hazel E. Barnes. New York: Philosophical, 1957.

Schultz, Elizabeth A. "The Heirs of Ralph Ellison: Patterns of Individualism in the Contemporary Afro-American Novel." *CLA Journal* 22 (1978): 101–22.

Shepperson, George. "Ethiopianism and African Nationalism." *Phylon* 13 (1953): 9–18.

Siskind, Aaron. *Harlem Document: Photographs 1932–1940.* Providence: Matrix, 1981.

Skerrett, Joseph T. "The Wright Interpretation: Ralph Ellison and the Anxiety of Influence." *Massachusetts Review* 21 (1980): 196–212.

Smith, Bessie. "Back Water Blues." Rec. 17 Feb. 1927. *Nobody's Blues But Mine.* Columbia, CG 31093, 1972.

Spanos, William V., ed. *A Casebook on Existentialism.* New York: Crowell, 1966.

Stendahl. *The Red and the Black.* 1830. Ed. and trans. Robert M. Adams. New York: Norton, 1969.

Stepto, Robert B. *From behind the Veil: A Study of Afro-American Narrative.* Urbana: U of Illinois P, 1979.

———. "Teaching Afro-American Literature: Survey or Tradition?" *Afro-American Literature: The Reconstruction of Instruction.* Ed. Dexter Fisher and Stepto. New York: MLA, 1979. 7–24.

Stepto, Robert B., and Michael Harper. "Study and Experience: An Interview with Ralph Ellison." *Chant of Saints: A Gathering of Afro-American Literature, Art, and Scholarship.* Ed. Stepto and Harper. Urbana: U of Illinois P, 1979. 451–69.

Sylvander, Carolyn. "Ralph Ellison's *Invisible Man* and Female Stereotypes." *Negro American Literature Forum* 9 (1975): 77–79.

Tischler, Nancy M. "Negro Literature and Classic Form." *Contemporary Literature* 10 (1969): 352–65.

Tocqueville, Alexis de. *Democracy in America.* 2 vols. 1835, 1840. Henry Reeve–Francis Bowen text. Ed. Phillips Bradley. New York: Knopf, 1945.

Torrance, Robert M. *The Comic Hero.* Cambridge: Harvard UP, 1978.

Trimmer, Joseph F., ed. *A Casebook on Ralph Ellison's* Invisible Man. New York: Crowell, 1972.

Tucker, Robert C., ed. *The Marx-Engels Reader.* 2nd ed. New York: Norton, 1978.

Turner, Darwin T. "Sight in *Invisible Man.*" *CLA Journal* 13 (1970): 258–64.

Tuveson, Ernest. *Redeemer Nation: The Idea of America's Millennial Role.* Chicago: U of Chicago P, 1968.

Twain, Mark. *Adventures of Huckleberry Finn*. 1884. Ed. Sculley Bradley, Richmond Croom Beatty, et al. 2nd ed. New York: Norton, 1977.

Unamuno, Miguel de. *The Agony of Christianity and Essays on Faith*. Vol. 5 of *Selected Works*.

———. *Our Lord Don Quixote: The Life of Don Quixote and Sancho with Related Essays*. Vol. 3 of *Selected Works*.

———. "Saint Manuel Bueno, Martyr." *Ficciones: Four Stories and a Play*. Vol. 7 of *Selected Works*. 133–80.

———. *Selected Works of Miguel de Unamuno*. Trans. Anthony Kerrigan. Ed. Anthony Kerrigan and Martin Nozick. 2nd ed. 7 vols. to date. Princeton: Princeton UP, 1967–   .

———. *The Tragic Sense of Life in Men and Nations*. Vol. 4 of *Selected Works*.

Vassilowitch, John, Jr. "Ellison's Dr. Bledsoe: Two Literary Sources." *Essays in Literature* 8.1 (1981): 109–13.

Walsh, Mary Ellen Williams. "*Invisible Man*: Ralph Ellison's Wasteland." *CLA Journal* 28 (1984): 150–58.

Washington, Booker T. *Up from Slavery*. Vol. 1 of *The Booker T. Washington Papers*. Ed. Louis R. Harlan and John W. Blassingame. Urbana: U of Illinois P, 1972. Rpt. in John Hope Franklin, *Three Negro Classics* 23–206.

Wells, H. G. *The Invisible Man*. 1897. Rpt. in *Best Science Fiction Stories of H. G. Wells*. New York: Dover, 1966. 1–110.

White, Timothy. *Catch a Fire: The Life of Bob Marley*. New York: Holt, 1983.

Whitman, Walt. Leaves of Grass: *Comprehensive Readers' Edition*. Ed. Harold W. Blodgett and Sculley Bradley. New York: New York UP, 1965.

Williams, Phillip G. "A Comparative Approach to Afro-American and Neo-African Novels: Ellison and Achebe." *Studies in Black Literature* 7.1 (1976): 15–18.

Wilner, Eleanor R. "The Invisible Black Thread: Identity and Nonentity in *Invisible Man*." *CLA Journal* 13 (1970): 242–57.

Wright, Richard. *American Hunger*. New York: Harper, 1977.

———. *Black Boy: A Record of Childhood and Youth*. New York: Harper, 1945.

———. "The Man Who Lived Underground." 1941. *Eight Men*. By Wright. New York: Pyramid, 1969. 22–74.

———. *Native Son*. New York: Harper, 1940.

———. "Richard Wright." *The God That Failed*. Ed. Richard Crossman. 1950. New York: Bantam, 1952. 115–62.

INDEX